RMP® Exam Question & Answer Preparation Guide

300 knowledge and situational questions with detailed solutions and rationale

Based on *Practice Standard for Project Risk Management* and *PMBOK® Guide* 5th Edition and (2016)

Foreword

Whenever you had to study a 'heavy' book, did you wish for a simpler guide just to get the gist of the subject? The objective of this guide is to give you a variety of sample exams that can help as you digest the heavier guides. This book is based on the thinking of having a crash course guide that you could go through and get a handle on the exam. As an experienced instructor, I always thought about and looked for such resources whenever I had to study a new subject or teaching a new subject. It was a similar feeling I had when I took up *Practice Standard for Project Risk Management* book to study. What I really wanted to know was what the Risk Management Professional (RMP®) exam is and how to answer the questions. This book will do that for you.

This is a guide on the RMP® exam questions and I will attempt to do three things in this book:

- Present you with a set of questions from the easy to the difficult
- Simulate the RMP® exam based on your knowledge and experience
- Explain the rationale and reasoning behind the RMP® questions

This exam question guide is based on the last 5 years of conducting RMP® workshops and understanding what it takes to build and prepare for the RMP® exam. This guide is made up of the easy to hard questions with the rationale that it is not about answering just the tough questions but also understanding the easy questions. I hope you enjoy the guide and find it useful to passing your RMP® exam

Table of Contents

How to Approach the RMP® Exam

Let's look at how to approach the Risk Management Professional (RMP®) exam questions. The best way of doing this, is through the analysis of a typical RMP® exam question

Question: You are the project manager of the YHG project for your company. Within the project, you and the project team have identified a risk event that could have a financial impact on the project of $450,000. This risk event has a 70 percent chance of occurring in the project. The project identifies a solution that will reduce the probability of the risk event to ten percent, but it will cost $260,000 to implement. Management agrees with the solution and asks that you include the risk response in the project plan. What risk response is this?

    A. This is mitigation because the response reduces the probability.
    B. This is not a risk response, but a change request.
    C. This is transference because of the $260,000 cost of the solution.
    D. This is avoidance because the risk response caused the project plan to be changed.

Go ahead, and choose an answer - A, B, C or D. Now, let us analyse the question

Question Analysis: If you look at the question – it is your knowledge of the various strategies that is important. You are been asked which is the best response strategy for the situation. The first step is to identify what you are doing and the best tool, approach or strategy to deal with it

Answer Analysis by Elimination: Now, let's look at the given choices to begin the elimination process.

- **Choice D** is avoidance. The approach of 'a solution that will reduce the probability of the risk event to ten percent, but it will cost $260,000 to implement' is not available as the project is actually trying to reduce the probability of this occurring
- **Choice C** is transference but there is no approach to getting the an external entity for the organisation or outside the organisation involved
- **Choice B** is invalid as 'the project a solution that will reduce the probability of the risk event to ten percent, but it will cost $260,000 to implement' is certainly a risk response
- **Choice A** is the correct answer as 'a solution that will reduce the probability of the risk event to ten percent, but it will cost $260,000 to implement' is certainly mitigation.

When you can understand the techniques, concepts and tool, the RMP exam is very doable. Choice A is the Best answer.

It is vital that you read PMI's® Practice Standard for Project Risk Management. The *Practice Standard for Project Risk Management* covers risk management as it is applied to single projects only. It does not cover risk in programs or portfolios. This practice standard is consistent with the PMBOK® Guide and is aligned with other PMI practice standards. Different projects, organizations and situations require a variety of approaches to risk management and there are several specific ways to conduct risk management that are in agreement with principles of Project Risk Management as presented in this practice standard.

Passing the RMP® Exam

To pass the RMP® exam, you need to have a good understanding of the five domain areas (described in this section).

Domain 1: - Risk and Strategy Planning

Activities related to developing policies, processes, and procedures for risk assessment, planning, and response.

Tasks	Risk Strategy and Planning (19 / 20%)
Task 1	Develop risk assessment processes and tools that quantify stakeholder risk tolerances in order to assess and determine risk thresholds for the project
Task 2	Update risk policies and procedures using information such as lessons learned from projects and outputs of risk audits in order to improve risk management effectiveness.
Task 3	Develop and recommend project risk strategy based on project objectives in order to establish the outline for the risk management plan.
Task 4	Produce risk management plan for the project on the basis of inputs such as project information, external factors, stakeholder inputs, and industry policies and procedures in order to define, fund, and staff effective risk management processes for the project that align with other project plans.
Task 5	Establish evaluation criteria for risk management processes based on project baselines and objectives in order to measure effectiveness of the project risk process.
	Knowledge of: • Continuous process improvement as applied to risk management • Knowledge management techniques for organizing and providing access to project risk information • Metrics for measuring effectiveness of project risk process • Risk attitude concepts • Risk Breakdown Structure (RBS) • Risk tolerance concepts • Barriers to effective risk management • Project risk management inputs, tools, techniques, and outputs • Project risk contingency and management reserve • Research and analysis techniques • Basic strategy development methodologies Skills in: • Assessing stakeholder risk tolerance and Building stakeholder consensus

Domain 2: - Stakeholder Engagement

Activities related to promoting the understanding of project risk management for stakeholders and project team members, assessing stakeholder risk tolerance, prioritising project risk, and promoting risk ownership.

Tasks	Stakeholder Engagement (19 / 20%)
Task 1	Promote a common understanding of the value of risk management by using interpersonal skills in order to foster an appropriate level of shared accountability, responsibility, and risk ownership.
Task 2	Train, coach, and educate stakeholders in risk principles and processes in order to create shared understanding of principles and processes, and foster engagement in risk management.
Task 3	Coach project team members in implementing risk processes in order to ensure the consistent application of risk processes.
Task 4	Assess stakeholder risk tolerance using processes and tools such as interviewing stakeholders and reviewing historical stakeholder behaviours in order to identify project risk thresholds.
Task 5	Identify stakeholder risk attitudes and cognitive biases using stakeholder analysis techniques in order to manage stakeholder expectations and responses throughout the life of the project.
Task 6	Engage stakeholders on risk prioritisation process based on stakeholder risk tolerance and other relevant criteria, in order to optimise consensus regarding priorities.
Task 7	Provide risk-related recommendations to stakeholders regarding risk strategy and planning, risk process facilitation, risk reporting, and specialised risk tasks by using effective communication techniques in order to support effective risk-based decision making
Task 8	Promote risk ownership by proactively communicating roles and responsibilities and engaging project team members in the development of risk responses in order to improve risk response execution.
Task 9	Liaise with stakeholders of other projects by using effective communication techniques and sharing information on project risk performance in order to inform them of implications for their projects.
	Knowledge of: • Information resources, both internal (for example, OPA) and external (for example, EEF) • Project performance information • Stakeholder sensitivity analysis models • Training and coaching techniques • Types of stakeholder risk attitudes (including but not limited risk seeking, risk tolerant, and risk averse) • Group decision making

- Group creativity (including but not limited to brainstorming, nominal group technique, Delphi technique, idea/mind mapping, and affinity diagram)

Skills in:

- Assessing stakeholder risk tolerance (appetite and attitude)
- Collaborating with stakeholders
- Managing teams

Domain 3: - Risk Process Facilitation

Activities related to facilitating risk identification, evaluation, prioritisation, and response among project team members.

Tasks	Risk Process Facilitation (25 / 28%)
Task 1	Apply risk assessment processes and tools in order to quantify stakeholder risk tolerances and determine risk levels.
Task 2	Facilitate risk identification using a variety of techniques in order to enable the project team and stakeholders to understand and determine the risk exposure of the project.
Task 3	Facilitate the project teams evaluation of the identified risks attributes using qualitative and quantitative tools and techniques in order to prioritise the risks for response planning
Task 4	Facilitate the development of an aligned risk response strategy and related risk actions by risk owners from the information gathered during risk analysis in order to ensure timely and defined action when required.
Task 5	Facilitate the formulation of project contingency reserve based on the risk exposure of the project in order to have the capability and resources to respond to realised risks.
Task 6	Provide risk data to cost and schedule analysts/estimators to ensure that project risk is properly reflected in cost and schedule estimates for the project.
Task 7	Use scenarios to validate potential risk responses and evaluate key dependencies and requirements in order to enhance the likelihood of project success.
	Knowledge of: <ul><li>Basic risk identification tools and techniques for both threats and opportunities (including but not limited to brainstorming, checklists, prompt lists, assumptions and constraints analysis, interviews, questionnaires, cause and effect analysis, SWOT analysis, document review, affinity diagrams, and lessons-learned review from similar projects)</li><li>Basic qualitative risk analysis tools and techniques (including but not limited to probability-impact matrices, risk scoring, Risk Breakdown Structure analysis, root cause analysis, Pareto prioritisation analysis, and risk metric trend analysis)</li><li>Basic quantitative risk analysis tools and techniques (including but not limited to Monte Carlo analysis, decision trees, FMEA/FMECA/Fault Tree analysis, and sensitivity analysis)</li><li>Heuristics and other dynamic sources of cognitive biases and their associated effects on risk perception and behavior</li><li>Risk response strategy types</li><li>Contingency management tools and techniques</li><li>Risk monitoring and control techniques</li><li>Group decision making</li></ul>

- Group creativity (including but not limited to brainstorming, nominal group technique, Delphi technique, idea/mind mapping, and affinity diagram)

Skills in:

- Using analytical software tools for project risk management
- Managing teams in multicultural environments
- Estimating probability and impact of identified risks

Domain 4: - Risk Monitoring and Reporting

Activities related to monitoring risk, evaluating risk response against established metrics, and communicating risk response performance to stakeholders and project team.

Tasks	Risk Monitoring and Reporting (19 / 20%)
Task 1	Document and periodically update project risk information using standard tools (including but not limited to risk register, risk database) and techniques in order to maintain a single, current repository of all project risk information.
Task 2	Coordinate with project manager using communication techniques in order to integrate risk management throughout the project.
Task 3	Create periodic standard and custom reports using risk-related metrics as specified in the risk management plan in order to communicate risk management activities and status.
Task 4	Monitor risk response metrics by analysing risk response performance information, and present to key stakeholders in order to ensure resolution of risk and develop additional risk response strategies to address residual and secondary risks.
Task 5	Analyse risk process performance against established metrics in order to drive risk process improvements.
Task 6	Update the project risk management plan using relevant internal and external inputs in order to keep the plan current.
Task 7	Capture risk lessons learned through comprehensive review of the project risk management plan, risk register, risk audits, risk process performance reports, and other associated reports in order to incorporate into future risk planning.
	Knowledge of: • Continuous process improvement and quality management as applied to risk management • Knowledge management techniques for organizing and providing access to project risk information • Alternative formats for project risk reports (for example, Top Risk List, • Risks Transitioned to Issues, Response Plans Behind Schedule, Risk • Triggers, and Risk Outcomes) • Requirements for risk register data fields • Risk statement construction • Risk response activity construction • Risk response metrics • Risk process performance metrics • Risk assessment analysis metrics • Risk management reserves (Note: There are no skills specific only to Domain 4)

Domain 5: - Perform Specialized Risk Activities

Activities related to the specialised quantitative and qualitative tools and techniques used by project risk management professionals.

Tasks	Perform Specialised Risk Activities (25 / 28%)
Task 1	Evaluate the attributes of identified risks using advanced quantitative tools and specialised qualitative techniques in order to estimate overall risk exposure of the project.
Task 2	Analyse risk data produced during the project using statistical analyses and expert judgment in order to determine strengths and weaknesses of risk strategy and processes and recommend process improvements when indicated.
Task 3	Perform specialised risk analysis using advanced tools and techniques in order to support stakeholder decision making for the project.
	Knowledge of: <ul><li>Advanced risk identification tools and techniques for both threats and opportunities (including but not limited to force field analysis, scenario planning, futures thinking, visualization, Delphi groups, and nominal group technique)</li><li>Advanced quantitative risk analysis tools and techniques (including but not limited to, integrated cost/schedule analysis, advanced Monte Carlo analysis, system dynamics, bowtie analysis, analytical hierarchy process, risk-based earned value analysis, risk-based critical chain analysis, and multi-factor regression analysis, modeling techniques, advanced risk metric analysis [including statistical process control])</li><li>Tools and techniques for identifying and analysing overall project risk (including but not limited to risk efficiency index, risk tolerance analysis, risk reserve analysis, risk metric trend analysis, risk taxonomy, risk connectivity analysis, Monte Carlo analysis against overall project objectives, project risk surveys, and correlation analysis)</li><li>Basic and advanced statistics</li><li>Estimation tools and techniques to support risk decision making (including but not limited to prioritisation, cost-benefit analysis, analogous, parametric, and bottom-up)</li><li>Advanced theory of heuristics and other sources of cognitive bias</li><li>Variance/Earned Value Analysis Skills</li><li>Skills in:</li><li>Converting qualitative information into risk data</li><li>Building representative risk models</li><li>Managing and interpreting quantitative and qualitative data</li></ul>

Answering from PMI's Perspective

The one major reason people get the answers wrong at the RMP® exam is that the questions are answered the exam questions from their own perspective, from their experience, of what they think is best. They do not answer the questions from PMI's perspective - of choosing from the best practice, and not from their current practice.

One of the major paradigm shift in the mind of the risk manager is to understand the *Practice Standard for Project Risk Management* and the *PMBOK® Guide*. Not all companies, countries, and project managers are operating from this level yet. But to know the highest standard is an eye opener already. Then you must use this high standard, the best practice to answer questions on the RMP® exam.

RMP® Exam Study Plan

Preparing for the RMP® exam requires a methodical plan, which must be followed with dedication. There is a certain amount of information that must be processed, understood, and applied on the exam questions.

There are a total of 5 Domain Areas and the RMP® exam is structured as follows:

Domain	% on test
Risk Strategy and Planning	20%
Stakeholder Engagement	20%
Risk Process Facilitation	25%
Risk Monitoring and Reporting	20%
Perform Specialized Risk Analysis	15%

To prepare for the RMP® exam, you need a step-by-step, methodical study plan that will make sure you set aside at least a short amount of time each day to study, and cover the entire material in smaller, byte sized segments. Most concepts are quite tactical and require some effort from the participant to understand, and apply to the exam. Attached is our Study Plan which is timed for a duration of three weeks.

Remaining Time	What to do	Focus	Objective
3 weeks to go			
Review the following chapters and take a batch of questions for each chapter Refer to the study guide when needed	Risk Management Overview	▪ Risk Management Process ▪ Understand Project Uncertainties ▪ Risks, Threats, and Opportunities ▪ Plan Risk Management Process ▪ Types of Risk	1. Take each chapter and ensure that you are familiar with the content / focus of that chapter. 2. It is not about retaining the information but to ensure that it makes sense and to identify the reason why PMI® are talking about particular items in these chapters 3. Take 10 - 20 questions per chapter 4. When answering the questions identify how many you are getting right and try to understand why you are getting the other wrong
	Before Beginning Risk Management	▪ Inputs to Risk Management ▪ Project Management Process ▪ Project Charter and Background Information ▪ Outputs from Project Planning ▪ Work Breakdown Structure ▪ Communication Management Plan	
	Risk Management Attitudes	▪ Stakeholder Management ▪ Risk Attitudes ▪ Risk Preference	
	Plan Risk Management	▪ Risk Team ▪ Risk Methodology ▪ Budget and Timing ▪ Definitions of Probability and Impact ▪ Report Formats and Tracking ▪ Roles and Responsibilities	
	Identify Risks	▪ Process of Identifying Risks ▪ Cause-Risk-Effect Format ▪ Checklists ▪ Brainstorming ▪ Expert Interviewing ▪ SWOT Technique	
1 week to go			
	Perform Qualitative Risk Analysis	▪ Qualitative Risk Analysis Process ▪ Tools & Techniques for Qualitative Analysis ▪ Motivational and Cognitive Bias ▪ Risk Rating, Ranking, and Score	1. Take each chapter and ensure that you are familiar with the content / focus of that chapter.

Review the following chapters and take a batch of questions for each chapter Refer to the study guide when needed	Perform Quantitative Risk Analysis	▪ What is Qualitative Risk Analysis? ▪ Methods to Quantitatively Assess Probability and Impact ▪ Monte Carlo Simulation ▪ Proving Likelihood of Project Completion ▪ Prioritising Risk Analysis	2. It is not about retaining the information but to ensure that it makes sense and to identify the reason why PMI® are talking about particular items in these chapters 3. Take 10 – 15 questions per chapter 4. When answering the questions identify how many you are getting right and try to understand why you are getting the other wrong
	Plan Risk Responses	▪ Methods for Reducing Overall Risk by Identifying Threats and Opportunities ▪ Responding to Negative Risk ▪ Planned Positive Risk Response ▪ Risk Response Plan ▪ Review Strategies	
	Monitor and Control Risks	▪ Methods for Monitoring & Measuring ▪ Taking Corrective Action ▪ Evaluating Effectiveness ▪ Issue Tracking	
	PMBOK® Process	▪ Plan Risk Management ▪ Identify Risks ▪ Perform Qualitative Risk Analysis ▪ Perform Quantitative Risk Analysis ▪ Plan for Risk Response ▪ Plan Project Procurements ▪ Plan Stakeholder Management	
1 week to go			
6 – 5 days	▪ Review the questions answered and which are your weakest area ▪ Review the Glossary of the *Practice Standard for Project Risk Management* ▪ Take a sample exam for Domain 1		
4 days	▪ Take another sample exam for Domain 2 and 3. For the questions you get wrong, analyse why. Identify the questions you are getting WRONG and why.		
3 days	▪ Take another sample exam and Domain 4 and 5. For the questions you get wrong, analyse why. Identify the questions you are getting WRONG and why.		

2 days	• Take the sample exam at the end of this book. For the questions you get wrong, analyse why. Focus on the 4 of the most difficult areas. Identify the questions you are getting WRONG and why.
1 day	• Time to relax and cover only the main points of concern
Exam Date.	

How to Use this Book

The sample exam are designed to be completed once you have completed a reference book (i.e. Practice Standard for Project Risk Management)

The sample exam has three sections:
1. The Answer Sheet: - This is where you can complete the exam.
2. The Exam itself
3. The Answers to the exam with rationale

This book offers you two sections of questions: -
1. Situational and Knowledge types RMP® questions based on the Risk Domain Areas. As you read your Study Guide, these question can be used to test your understanding
2. A dedicated Knowledge based RMP® sample exam. The objective of this exam is to find out how well you know the Practice Standard for Project Risk Management. This exam should be done when you feel you have fully completed the review of your Study Guide

RMP® Sample Exam per Domain Area

Domain 1: - Risk and Strategy Planning Exam

Answer Sheet

Question	Answer	Correction		Question	Answer	Correction
1				21		
2				22		
3				23		
4				24		
5				25		
6				26		
7				27		
8				28		
9				29		
10				30		
11				31		
12				32		
13				33		
14				34		
15				35		
16				36		
17				37		
18				38		
19				39		
20				40		

Exam

1   The Project Risk Management knowledge area does not focus on which of the following processes?

A. Quantitative Risk Analysis
B. Risk Monitoring and Control
C. Potential Risk Monitoring
D. Risk Management Planning

2   Management tells a project manager to subcontract part of the project to a company that management has worked with many times. Under these circumstances, the project manager should be MOST concerned about:

A. Making sure the company has the qualifications to complete the project.
B. Meeting management expectations of time.
C. The cost of the subcontracted work.
D. The contract terms and conditions.

3   A project manager discovers an urgent need for outsourced resources on the project. He knows he has the money to cover the cost of these resources. He goes to the procurement manager and explains the situation, insisting a contract be drawn up today so he can obtain resources and circumvent the standard procedure. Is this the correct process to follow?

A. Yes, of course. For urgent needs, it is not necessary to follow the organisation's procedure regarding procurement.
B. Yes. Urgent needs from projects should always be dealt with immediately as directed by the project manager.
C. No. The procurement manager has a process to follow when creating contracts that helps protect the company and its projects.
D. No. The procurement manager should be checking in with the project manager to see if he is in need of a contract, rather than making the project manager come and ask for one.

4   You are the project manager of the GHY project for your organisation. You are about to start the qualitative risk analysis process for the project and you need to determine the roles and responsibilities for conducting risk management. Where can you find this information?

A. Enterprise environmental factors
B. Risk register
C. Risk management plan
D. Staffing management plan

5   Tom works as a project manager for BlueWell Inc. He is determining which risks can affect the project. Which of the following inputs of the identify risks process is useful in identifying risks, and provides a quantitative assessment of the likely cost to complete the scheduled activities?
     A. Activity cost estimates
     B. Cost management plan
     C. Activity duration estimates
     D. Risk management plan

6   You are in the middle of developing risk assessment processes and tools that can quantify stakeholder risk tolerances in order to assess and determine risk thresholds for the project. This is core activity for the risk manager and incorporate the help of other to achieve this. What is a core tool and technique to achieve this?
     A. Delphi Technique
     B. Risk Breakdown Structure
     C. Stakeholder Sensitivity Analysis Models
     D. Group Decision Making

7   You are the project manager for an upcoming project. You're working on the procurement plan for the program that will control the IT aspect of the project. You've decided to contract with a professional services company that specialises in writing custom software programs. You want to minimise the risk to the organisation, so you'll opt for which contract type?
     A. Fixed price plus incentive
     B. Cost plus fixed fee
     C. Fixed price
     D. Cost plus incentive

8   Andrew has joined as the Project Manager of a project. One of the project documents available to Andrew lists down all the risks in a hierarchical fashion. What is this document called?
     A. Risk Management Plan.
     B. List of risks.
     C. Monte Carlo diagram.
     D. Risk Breakdown Structure

9   Jim updates risk policies and procedures using information such as lessons learned from projects and outputs of risk audits in order to improve the risk management effectiveness with HJK Inc. Jim is unaware of certain performances of the project which he has not captured. Why could have this happened to Jim's project?
     A. The project did not assess stakeholder tolerances
     B. The risk management process was not known within the organisation
     C. Metrics for measuring effectiveness of project risk process were not known
     D. The project performed the lesson learnt too early

10   Which of the following statements is true about risks?
A. When evaluating risks their impact should be considered, however probability of occurrence is not important.
B. Risks if they happen always have negative impact and not positive.
C. Risk register documents all the risks in detail.
D. Risk response plan is another name for Risk Management Plan.

11   Which of the following statements regarding reserve time (contingency) is false?
A. Contingency may be added to the activity duration or elsewhere in the schedule as recognition of a schedule risk.
B. Adding reserve time to the majority of the project activities is preferred and recommended.
C. The reserve time may be reduced or eliminated once more precise information about the project becomes available.
D. Reserve time should be documented along with other data and assumptions.

12   You are assigned as the project manager in a project with an aggressive schedule. During a recent meeting your team complained about the high pressure applied and the many hours of overwork time. What is the preferred solution to handle the problem?
A. Try to obtain additional budget and time.
B. Improve team communication and availability of high quality data on risks. Use this information to enable you to make well-founded decisions earlier.
C. The problem might be the customer disturbing project rhythm. Keep him on distance from the team.
D. Apply fast tracking to shorten project duration without additional work.

13   In order to complete work on your projects, you have been provided confidential information from all of your clients. A university contacts you to help it in its research. Such assistance would require you to provide the university with some of the client data from your files. What should you do?
A. Release the information, but remove all references to the clients' names.
B. Provide high-level information only.
C. Contact your clients and seek permission to disclose the information.
D. Disclose the information.

14   Fred is the project manager of a large project in his organisation. Fred needs to begin planning the risk management plan with the project team and key stakeholders. Which plan risk management process tool and technique should Fred use to plan risk management?
A. Variance and trend analysis
B. Information gathering techniques
C. Planning meetings and analysis
D. Data gathering and representation techniques

15 Henry is the project manager of the QBG Project for his company. This project has a budget of $4,576,900 and is expected to last 18 months to complete. The CIO, a stakeholder in the project, has introduced a scope change request for additional deliverables as part of the project work and to ensure all risks can be mitigated. What component of the change control system would review the proposed impact on the features and functions of the project's product to understand the level of risk?
A. Scope change control system
B. Cost change control system
C. Configuration management system
D. Integrated change control

16 Planning meetings and analysis is a tool and technique of which process?
A. Perform Qualitative Risk Analysis
B. Perform Quantitative Risk Analysis
C. Plan Risk Management
D. Monitor and Control Risks

17 Frank is the project manager of the NHH Project. He is working with the project team to create a plan to document the procedures to manage risks throughout the project. This document will define how risks will be identified and quantified. It will also define how contingency plans will be implemented by the project team. What document is Frank and the NHH Project team creating in this scenario?
A. Resource management plan
B. Project plan
C. Project management plan
D. Risk management plan

18 Who has the cost risk in a fixed price (FP) contract?
A. Team
B. Buyer
C. Seller
D. Management

19 Frank is the project manager of the NHL Project for his company and he is starting the risk identification process for the project. Frank needs to ensure that the correct stakeholders are interviewed as part of risk identification. What document will help Frank to communicate and solicit inputs of the project stakeholders during risk identification?
A. Project charter
B. Risk register
C. Requirements management plan
D. Stakeholder register

20   Your organisation has named you the project manager of the JKN Project. This project
     has a BAC of $1,500,000 and it is expected to last 18 months. Management has agreed
     that if the schedule baseline has a variance of more than five percent then you will need
     to crash the project. What happens when the project manager crashes a project?
     A. Project risks will increase.
     B. The project will take longer to complete, but risks will diminish.
     C. Project costs will increase.
     D. The amount of hours a resource can be used will diminish.

21   John works as a project manager for ABD project. He and his team, are working on the
     following activities:
     - Relative ranking of a priority list of project risks
     - Watchlist of low priority risk
     - Trends in Qualitative Risk Analysis results
     In which of the following processes is John working on?
     A. Perform Qualitative Risk Analysis
     B. Plan Risk Management
     C. Plan Risk Responses
     D. Perform Quantitative Risk Analysis

22   A project manager of a retail chain of hardware stores is in the process of conducting
     risk identification activities. In considering the potential risks, he and his team identified
     55 risks total. During a planning meeting, a discussion was held on a particular risk
     identified, which involves potential lawsuits if a customer or employee were to get
     injured from the display of chainsaws. What type of risk is this?
     A. Business Risk
     B. Pure Risk
     C. Partial Risk
     D. Organisational Risk

23   One of the outputs of the perform qualitative risk analysis is risk register updates. When
     the project manager updates the risk register he will need to include several pieces of
     information including all of the following except for which one?
     A. Trends in qualitative risk analysis
     B. Risk probability-impact matrix
     C. Watchlist of low-priority risks
     D. Risks grouped by categories

24   All of the following are common results of risk management EXCEPT?
     A. Contract terms and conditions are created.
     B. The project management plan is changed.
     C. The communications management plan is changed.
     D. The project charter is changed.

25   What project management plan is most likely to direct the quantitative risk analysis
      process for a project in a matrix environment?
      A. Risk analysis plan
      B. Staffing management plan
      C. Human resource management plan
      D. Risk management plan

26   Where can a project manager find project risk responsibilities?
      A. Risk management plan
      B. Organisational process assets
      C. Enterprise environmental factors
      D. Risk probability and impact matrix

27   Where can a project manager find risk-rating rules?
      A. Risk management plan
      B. Organisational process assets
      C. Enterprise environmental factors
      D. Risk probability and impact matrix

28   During which risk management process is a determination to transfer a risk made?
      A. Risk identification
      B. Quantitative risk analysis
      C. Risk response planning
      D. Risk monitoring and control

29   You have just started administrating a contract when management decides to terminate
      the contract based on the risk. What should you do FIRST?
      A. Go back to request seller responses.
      B. Go back to plan contracting.
      C. Finish contract administration.
      D. Go to contract closure.

30   Risk strategy and planning is based on which of the following tools and techniques
      A. Development of a risk management plan
      B. Continuous process improvement
      C. Qualitative and quantitative tools and techniques
      D. Risk response and control tool

31   When a project is assessing stakeholder risk tolerance and building stakeholder
      consensus, what activity is being performed?
      A. Developing risk assessment processes
      B. Developing risk identification processes
      C. Developing risk response processes
      D. Developing risk control processes

32   Kelly is the project manager of the NNQ Project for her company. This project will last for one year and has a budget of $350,000. Kelly is working with her project team and subject matter experts to begin the risk response planning process. When the project manager begins the plan risk response process, what two inputs will she need?
A. Risk register and the risk response plan
B. Risk register and power to assign risk responses
C. Risk register and the risk management plan
D. Risk register and the results of risk analysis

33   Your program manager has come to you, the project manager, for help with a bid for her newest project. You want to protect your company from financial risk. You have limited scope definition. What is the BEST type of contract to choose?
A. Fixed price (FP)
B. Cost plus percent of cost (CPPC)
C. Time and material (T&M)
D. Cost plus fixed fee (CPFF)

34   Which of the following statements regarding pure risk is true
A. The risk can be deflected or transferred to another party through a contract or insurance policy
B. Pure risk involve the chance of both a profit and a loss
C. No opportunities are associated with pure risk, only threats
D. Pure risk could be classified as a known-unknown risk

35   You want to develop and establish evaluation criteria for risk management processes based on project baselines and objectives in order to measure effectiveness of the project risk process. What tool and technique should be used to do this?
A. Strategy development methodologies
B. Risk identification tools
C. Decision trees
D. Stakeholder analysis tools

36   An experienced project manager has just begun working for a large information technology integrator. Her manager provides her with a draft project charter and immediately asks her to provide an analysis of the risks on the project. Which of the following would BEST help in this effort?
A. An article from PM Network Magazine
B. Her project scope statement from the project planning process
C. Her resource plan from the project planning process
D. A conversation with a team member from a similar project that failed in the past

37   Your project is in middle of managing the contract, when the seller comes to you to discuss some of the items of the RFP. The seller has a series of questions that need to be discussed and want to set up meeting with you and your project team. You investigate the items and agree that a discussion should happen. What should you say to the seller?
A. Let us sit down and discuss all changes and come to an agreeable conclusion
B. The changes should be benchmarked against the contract and not the RFP
C. Examine the contract to see what legal rights the seller has to issue claims against the contract
D. Inform the seller that the contract and RFP are agreed and not open for discussion

38   You have replaced an earlier project manager in a project .The earlier project manager has left the organisation and you are now responsible for the project. On reviewing the project management plan you are disturbed because a number of procurement contracts have been signed and they all turn out to be Cost plus fixed fee types of contracts - why are you worried?
A. All the risk is now with the seller
B. Contracts should always be T and M
C. Seller has no motivation to control cost and in fact cost could spiral
D. Contracts should always be Fixed Price

39   A particular stakeholder has a reputation for making numerous changes on the project. The project manager is concerned with this situation as the project needs to be managed against an agreed timeline and budget. What should the project manager do at the beginning of the project to manage this situation?
A. Say 'NO' to the stakeholder to dissuade him from submitting changes
B. Talk to the stakeholder's boss and persuade her that the stakeholder should be directed to another project
C. Get the stakeholder involved in the project as early as possible
D. Ask the stakeholder to be reasonable and if not, they are not to be included in the stakeholder register

40   When is passive risk acceptance an appropriate approach?
A. When the likeliness of risk occurrence is very low.
B. When the risk occurrence is hard to identify.
C. When it is best to deal with a risk as it occurs.
D. When the risk cannot be assessed or analysed.

Answers

1 C This should be simple question in that Option C is not part of the risk management plan

2 A The main fallout is that the project has being unable to perform the 'Conduct Procurement' process which means they have been unable to evaluate the sub-contractors. Okay the sub-contractor is known to the organisation but the sun-contractor should be evaluated with respect to THIS contract.

3 C Process must be followed is the simple explanation. Yes it is urgent, and resources are needed and while such things can be fast-tracked (which is not given in the options), you must at all times abide by process.

4 C The risk management roles and responsibilities are contained in the risk management plan. This is where all the risk management process information is contained

5 A The key part of this questions is that you are assessing cost impacts to the schedule. Hence the BEST answer is Option A which are the cost estimates

6 B The answer here is a Risk Breakdown Structure and this is a core tool and technique for strategic and risk planning. These are activities related to developing policies, processes, and procedures for risk assessment, planning, and response.

7 C The question is in the final sentence 'You want to minimise the risk to the organisation, so you'll opt for which contract type?' In PMI contract terms (as a buyer or project manager), the best way of eliminating risk (using contractual methods) is through a fixed price contract whereby the risk is transferred to the seller.

8 D Hierarchical description of risks is called Risk Breakdown structure.

9 C This is a tough risk question and is concerned with understanding why the project missed some key information. The reason for this is that the correct metrics for measuring effectiveness of project risk process were not available

10 C Risk register documents the risks in detail.

11 B This question is asking you for the 'FALSE' answer. The first thing to note is that reserve time is identified as contingency and this can be defined as the time / money that is added to a project to manage the known-unknowns. Choice A, D and C all revolve around the management of contingency whereas Choice B while valid is not necessarily correct as it would involve presenting contingency to all activities in the schedule.

12 A You must work for the good of the team and in this case, option A is the best one. All other options are destructive towards the team.

13 C Confidential information should be respected (not disclosed to third parties without the express approval of the client). If you picked choice A, remember that the clients own the confidential information. See, not all professional and social responsibility questions are tough!

14 C Option A, B and D are either risk analysis or identification tools. The question is asking for risk management planning tools which in this case is Option C

15 C This is not necessarily a risk management question but more to do with the system to manage risk information. The correct answer here is Configuration Management as this encompasses the systems required to manage project information

16 C You can argue that meetings are valid for all options. However, planning meetings and analysis are a core part of the risk management planning process

17 D The question is asking which document will shows ' how risks will be identified and quantified'. There is only one document that can do this and this is the Risk Management Plan which is Option D

18 C The first to do is identify that the buyer is the project and the seller is the vendor / contractor. This terminology discounts answer A and D. Anything that is fixed price is a risk for the seller and answer C should be chosen as it is the tightest type of contract from a buyer's perspective

19 D This is more a PMBOK question but again it focuses on risk. If you examine the question, it asks 'What document will help Frank to communicate and solicit inputs of the project stakeholders during risk identification'. The only stakeholder analysis tool is the stakeholder register

20 C Let's first explain what crashing is ... this is the reduction of the scheduled duration of the project based on an increase in cost or resources. With this definition, the answer has to be Option C

21 A The three elements should give away the answer:
      - Relative ranking of a priority list of project risks
      - Watchlist of low priority risk
      - Trends in Qualitative Risk Analysis results
      The answer is Qualitative Analysis

22 A This is an example of business risk as the risk itself can impact the business and the association with the customer. It is not Pure risk (as this is both positive and negative). There is a strong claim that this could be an organisational risk but this risk does not involve organisational strategies or processes

23   B   The risk register does not include the probability / impact matrix. This is an element of the risk management plan. The risk register will include: -
- Trends in qualitative risk analysis
- Watchlist of low-priority risks
- Risks grouped by categories

24   D   A change to the project charter is not always necessary. In fact, a change to the charter is a fundamental change to the project and may require a major adjustment to all aspects of the project management plan. There are many reasons the other choices could happen as a result of risk. Since a contract can only be created after risks are known (a contract is a tool to transfer risks) it is common sense that choice A cannot be the exception. The project management plan (choice B) could change to include a modified WBS and new work packages related to mitigating risk. The communications management plan (choice C) could change as a way to address a risk. Choice D is the best answer.

25   D   There is one risk management plan as part of the risk process and yes it is called a risk management plan. If you are not getting these questions right, I would ask you to go back to the standard and make sure you are comfortable with the definitions, tools and techniques

26   B   Project risk responsibilities are part of the risk management plan. While they originate with the Organisational Process Assets, the actual project risk responsibilities are contained in the risk management plan

27   B   Risk-rating rules should be part of the corporate knowledge and are used to develop the risk management plan

28   C   Transference is a risk response strategy.

29   D   If the contract is terminated, the project needs to enter closure. You need those results for historical purposes.

30   B   One of the knowledge areas for risk management strategy and planning is continuous process improvement as applied to risk management

31   A   When you re-look at this question, it is pretty straightforward. The project is assessing stakeholder tolerances which is pure assessment activities

32   C   The question asks as the project manager begins the plan risk response process, what two inputs are needed.
- the risk response plan is an output - this excludes Option A
- the results of the risk analysis will be part of the risk register - this excludes Option D
The power to assign risk responses is the same as understanding the risk responsibilities and this is part of the risk management plan. Hence Option C is the BETTER answer

33   D   Of the options given, the only contract that limits fees for large projects with limited scope definition is CPFF.

34   B   Pure risk is both positive and negative and hence choice B is correct. Remember this definition

35   A   This is a question on how to develop a risk approach. The best answer is A as it focuses on strategy and development whereas the other choices are specific to particular elements of the risk management process

36   D   Option D is an example of historical records / lessons learnt which is valid

37   B   The key part of this question is to identify where this situation happens and this is when the contract is been managed. So we must assume that a contract does exist. The seller has every right to discuss items but the discussion should be benchmarked against the Contract and not the RFP. Hence Choice B is correct

38   C   As a project manager - you indeed have a reason to be worried if your project has already signed off on Cost Plus Fee type of contracts. This is because in such contracts - you the buyer needs to pay the seller for all the costs and in addition an agreed percentage of the cost. As a result there is no motivation on the seller to control the costs - in fact it is in the interest of the seller to increase the costs. It is not necessary that all projects should always be T and M or Fixed Price. Option A is clearly wrong since all the risks are in fact with the buyer not the seller! The correct answer is Option C

39   C   The stakeholder cannon be avoided and should be working with to get the best possible outcome for the stakeholder and the project (Choice C)

40   A   Option B and D indicates that it should not be a risk. Option C indicates that acceptance may not be the most appropriate option. Hence option A remains

Domain 2: - Stakeholder Engagement Exam

Answer Sheet

Question	Answer	Correction	Question	Answer	Correction
1			21		
2			22		
3			23		
4			24		
5			25		
6			26		
7			27		
8			28		
9			29		
10			30		
11			31		
12			32		
13			33		
14			34		
15			35		
16			36		
17			37		
18			38		
19			39		
20			40		

Exam

1   Which of the following are principles and processes in order to create a shared understanding of principles and processes, and foster engagement in risk management?
   A. Training, coaching and educating stakeholders
   B. Diversity and cultural understanding
   C. Brainstorming and workshop activities
   D. Process mapping and brainstorming

2   A risk manager had just been hired to take over risk management responsibilities for a company producing a new pharmaceutical drug for diabetics. During the first cycle of risk identification, it was determined that the project had a high level of risk, and an expert was needed. The risk manager's first order of business is to look over the risk management plan. All of the following are most likely to be addressed within the plan EXCEPT:
   A. Stakeholder risk tolerances
   B. Budget for risk activities
   C. Definitions of risk probability and impact
   D. Risk owners

3   You are the project manager of the CUL project in your organisation. You and the project team are assessing the risk events and creating a probability and impact matrix for the identified risks. Which one of the following statements best describes the requirements for developing a probability and impact matrix?
   A. A focus on stakeholder commitment to project risk management
   B. A focus on stakeholder contribution to define risk responsibilities in managing the probability and impact matrix
   C. A focus on stakeholder commitment to issue and contingency resolution
   D. A focus on stakeholder contribution to understand probability and impact scales

4   Which tools are used to assess stakeholder risk tolerances?
   A. Process mapping
   B. Decision Trees
   C. Interviews and reviews
   D. Brainstorming

5   You are conducting Stakeholder Analysis. Which of the following questions can help you draw out stakeholder interests?
   A. Are there any conflicting interests that the stakeholder may have with the project?
   B. How committed is the stakeholder to the project? Is he/she willing to commit tangible resources?
   C. Are there relationship conflicts between stakeholders that can hinder the project?
   D. All of the above

6   Stakeholder management includes which of the following?
    A. Allowing stakeholder involvement in planning; allowing project managers focus on managing engagement and managing information to / from stakeholders
    A. Defining stakeholder identification and management techniques; allowing project managers to spend more time on project planning and managing information to / from stakeholders
    A. Presenting stakeholder reports; allowing project managers focus on managing engagement and managing information to stakeholders
    A. Defining stakeholder identification and management techniques; allowing project managers focus on managing engagement and managing information to / from stakeholders

7   You are a project manager for a new Natural Project. You have just completed and obtained sign-off on the scope statement for your product. The stakeholder has informed you that a deliverable is missing from the scope statement. This deliverable is a critical success factor. You should do which of the following?
    A. Inform the stakeholder that work not stated in the scope statement is excluded from the project.
    B. Modify the scope statement to reflect the new deliverable.
    C. Inform the stakeholder that this deliverable can be included in the next project since sign-off has already been obtained.
    D. Modify the scope statement after an approved change request has been received from the stakeholder.

8   Identifying risk tolerance is a vital part of the risk management process. There are many reasons why this should be performed. Which of the following is the core reason why risk tolerances should be identified?
    A. To change stakeholder expectations and responses throughout the life of the project
    B. To determine cognitive biases for stakeholder assessment
    C. To explain cognitive biases for stakeholder assessment
    D. To manage stakeholder expectations and responses throughout the life of the project

9   You work as a project manager for BlueWell Inc. You are working with Jon, the CIO of your company, on several risks within the project. Jon understands that through quantitative analysis you have used decision tress to understand and evaluate different risk and options. Jon's concern, however, is that the impact and probability of these risk events may change as conditions within the project may change. He would like to know what you are going to do?
    A. Perform further analysis with the decision trees
    B. Do assumptions analysis to understand the risk basis
    C. Perform Monte Carlo analysis to define the variations
    D. Identify the risks that could impact the outcome

10 When assessing the level of stakeholder engagement, which of the following analytical techniques should be used?
A. Unaware of the project and impact
B. Focused on project engagement and planning
C. Resistant is aware of the project but resistant to change
D. Neutral and is neither supportive nor resistant

11 Risk tolerances are determined in order to help:
A. the team rank the project risks.
B. the project manager estimate the project.
C. the team schedule the project.
D. management know how other managers will act on the project.

12 A major negotiation with a potential supplier is scheduled for the next day when you discover that the project may get cancelled due to the risk and exposure. What should you do?
A. Spend as little time as necessary in preparing for the negotiations.
B. Only negotiate major items.
C. Go ahead as planned as there is still a chance that the project may continue.
D. Postpone the negotiations for now.

13 Which of these statements about Risk in a project is correct?
A. A risk is always induced external to the project.
B. Risks need not be planned for in all projects
C. Risks are always negative in nature and are threats that need to be managed well
D. Risk responses reflect an organisation's perceived balance between risk taking and risk avoidance

14 Your project sponsor has asked you to present your project's high-level risk register to him in the next project update meeting. Which of the following processes must be started to have your high level risk register?
A. Identify Risks
B. Perform Qualitative Risk Analysis
C. Plan Risk Management
D. Control Risks

15 As the project manager, of a project to construct a city park, you have yourself identified 39 risks on the project, determined what would trigger the risks, rated them on a risk rating matrix, tested the assumptions and assessed the quality of the data used. You now plan to move to the next step of the risk management process. What have you missed?
A. Overall risk ranking for the project
B. Simulation
C. Involvement of other stakeholders
D. Risk Mitigation

16   Which of the following is true about risks?
      A. The risk register documents all the identified risks in detail
      B. Risk impact should be considered, but probability of occurrence is not important
      C. Risks always have negative impact and not positive
      D. Risk Response Plan is another name for Risk Management Plan.

17   Your status meetings have project stakeholders from various parts of the globe. Which
      of the following is best to avoid communication errors during the meeting?
      A. Use teleconferencing and send the meeting notes.
      B. Ask the stakeholders in your geography to stay on the call and tell the others that the
      meetings notes will be distributed to them via email.
      C. Create the communication plan.
      D. Exercise active listening and use video conferencing

18   Negotiations between two parties are becoming complex, so party A makes some notes
      that both parties sign. However, when the work is being done, party B claims that they
      are not required to provide an item they both agreed to during negotiations, because it
      was not included in the subsequent contract. In this case, party B is:
      A. Incorrect, because both parties must comply with what they agreed upon.
      B. Correct, because there was an offer.
      C. Generally correct, because both parties are only required to perform what is in the
      contract.
      D. Generally incorrect, because all agreements must be upheld.

19   The project manager and project sponsor are discussing the project costs and whether
      it is better to have their own company do part of the project or hire another company to
      do the work. If they asked for your opinion, you might say it would be better to do the
      work yourself if:
      A. There is a lot of proprietary data.
      B. You have the expertise but you do not have the available manpower.
      C. You do not need control over the work.
      D. Your company resources are limited.

20   You have being assigned to a project that is not going very well. You have discussed
      the project with the sponsor and have agreed that there is a need to change some of
      the core requirements of the project. The sponsor is committed to the action and has
      requested the functional managers to support the project. As the project manager, what
      should you do NEXT?
      A. Meet with the team and brainstorm the requirements to be changed
      B. Focus on the project budget to understand what the variations are and how they will
      be managed
      C. Meet with the customer to understand the requirement changes and how they are
      impacted
      D. Have a project meeting with all stakeholder to kick-off the project

21 All of the following statements are true EXCEPT:
    A. Influence diagrams are a diagramming technique used within risk identification.
    B. Stakeholders can participate in brainstorming and interviewing sessions.
    C. The Delphi Technique utilises anonymous participation from stakeholders to evaluate important risk information.
    D. Cause and effect diagrams are also known as Ishikawa diagrams and fishbone diagrams.

22 You have discovered that a new pipeline project you are managing may pose a threat to the environment. What is the most appropriate action?
    A. Seek guidance from government officials.
    B. Contact the media and be open re your discovery.
    C. Get advice from an attorney.
    D. Resign from the project.

23 You have been appointed as the manager of a new, large, and complex project. Because this project is business-critical and very visible, senior management has told you to analyse the project's risks and prepare response strategies for them as soon as possible. The organisation has risk management procedures that are seldom used or followed, and has had a history of handling risks badly. The project's first milestone is in two weeks. In preparing the risk response plan, input from which of the following is generally LEAST important?
    A. Project team members
    B. Project sponsor
    C. Individuals responsible for risk management policies and templates
    D. Key stakeholders

24 Which of the following techniques would a project use to provide risk-related recommendations to stakeholders regarding risk strategy and planning, risk process facilitation, risk reporting and specialised risk tasks?
    A. Effective communication techniques
    B. Decision making techniques
    C. Stakeholder engagement techniques
    D. Wideband Delphi techniques

25 You are working on a construction project. You, your team, and your senior manager all feel that the work is complete. However, one of your stakeholders disagrees, and feels that one deliverable is not acceptable due to the risk exposure. What is the BEST way to handle this conflict?
    A. Consult the contract and follow its claims administration procedure
    B. Renegotiate the contract
    C. File a lawsuit to force the stakeholder to accept the deliverable
    D. Follow the administrative and contract closure procedures

26   You are the project manager for BlueWell Inc. Your current project is a high priority and
high profile project within your organisation. You want to identify the project
stakeholders that will have the most power in relation to their interest on your project.
This will help you plan for project risks, stakeholder management, and ongoing
communication with the key stakeholders in your project. In this process of stakeholder
analysis, what type of a grid or model should you create based on these conditions?
A. Stakeholder power/interest grid
B. Influence/impact grid
C. Salience model
D. Stakeholder register

27   Depending on the project, the conditions, and the potential for loss or reward,
stakeholders will have differing tolerances for risk. Which of the following best describes
the relationship between the time and costs required to eliminate the chance of failure
and the stakeholder's risk tolerance level?
A. The time and money costs required to eliminate the chance of failure is not related to
the stakeholders' level of risk tolerance.
B. The time and money costs required to eliminate the chance of failure is much higher
than the stakeholders' level of risk tolerance.
C. The time and money costs required to eliminate the chance of failure is much lower
than the stakeholders' level of risk tolerance.
D. The time and money costs required to eliminate the chance of failure is in proportion
to the stakeholders' tolerance of risk on the project.

28   You have just taken control of a large-scale project of architectural engineering, and one
of the sponsors reminds you of another important yet trouble-making stakeholder
notorious for requesting changes. You have dealt with this stakeholder in the past and
while it has being tough going, you have generally reached a successful outcome with
him. This project is considered by one of the key projects in the organisations portfolio
and do not want any obstacles along the project path. As a project manager, how would
you best deal with this potential stakeholder problem?
A. Ignore this stakeholder's change requests.
B. Get the stakeholder involved and participating from the initiating process.
C. Ask the stakeholder to reduce their change requests through the stakeholder's
manager.
D. Ask your manager to talk to this stakeholder about the repercussions of excessive
change requests.

29   A project manager discovers an urgent needs for outsourced resources on the project. He knows he has the capital for the resources and goes to the procurement manager to explain the situation. He insists that a letter of intent is drawn up as soon as possible so he can obtain the resources and move forward without having to get caught in red tape. What would you recommend to the project manager: -
A. Continue as this an urgent request and organisation policies and procedures do not need to be adhered to in such situations
B. Continue as urgent requests need immediate action
C. Do not continue as the procurement manager has a process that must be followed
D. Do not continue as it is the role of the procurement manager to initiate such requests rather than the project manager

30   A project manager reviewing a control chart noticed that three of the processes were climbing up towards the upper control limit. What should the project manager do?
A. Investigate what is causing the processes to move in this direction.
B. Nothing, since the processes are within the control limits.
C. Do everything possible to prevent the future processes from following the trend.
D. Follow up with the quality department to see what they are doing about it, since this shows potential risks.

31   A contractor is working on a fixed price contract that calls for a single, lump sum payment upon satisfactory completion of the contract. About halfway through the contract, the contractor's project manager informs their contract administrator that financial problems are making it difficult for them to pay their employees and subcontractors. The contractor asks for a partial payment for work accomplished. Which of the following actions by the buyer is most likely to cause problems for the project?
A. Starting partial payments for work accomplished.
B. Making no payments because it would violate the conditions of the contract.
C. Paying for work accomplished to date.
D. Negotiating a change to the payment conditions in the contract.

32   You are finalising the monthly project status report due now to your manager when you discover that several project team members are not reporting actual hours spent on project activities. This results in skewed project statistics. What is the MOST appropriate action to be taken?
A. Discuss the impacts of these actions with team members.
B. Report the team members' actions to their functional managers.
C. Continue reporting information as it is presented to you.
D. Provide accurate and truthful information at all time.

33 As a project manager, you realise that handling Project Stakeholder expectations is an important priority. Which statement regarding project stakeholders is not correct?
A. Negative stakeholders must be ignored if the project has to be brought to a successful completion.
B. Stakeholders have varying levels of responsibility and authority when participating on a project and these can change over the project's life cycle.
C. Some key stakeholders include project manager, performing organisation, project team members, customer and sponsor.
D. Stakeholder expectations may be difficult to manage because stakeholders often have conflicting objectives.

34 A project manager currently working on a mid-level pharmaceutical project was in the process of developing the list of identified risks. Risk experts were brought into the process, who provided feedback anonymously. The project manager utilised this technique to avoid bias in the responses and feedback provided by the risk experts. Which of the following techniques is the project manager utilising?
A. Brainstorming
B. SWOT Analysis
C. Delphi Technique
D. Interviewing

35 Shelly is the project manager of the BUF project for her company. In this project Shelly needs to establish some rules to reduce the influence of risk bias during the qualitative risk analysis process. What method can Shelly take to best reduce the influence of risk bias?
A. Group stakeholders according to positive and negative stakeholders and then complete the risk analysis
B. Determine the risk root cause rather than the person identifying the risk events
C. Establish risk boundaries
D. Establish definitions of the level of probability and impact of risk event

36 You are the project manager for your organisation. You are working with your key stakeholders in the qualitative risk analysis process. You understand that there is certain bias towards the risk events in the project that you need to address, manage, and ideally reduce. What solution does the PMBOK recommend to reduce the influence of bias during qualitative risk analysis?
A. Establish the definitions of the levels of probability and impact
B. Provide iterations of risk analysis for true reflection of a risk probability and impact
C. Isolate the stakeholders by project phases to determine their risk bias
D. Involve all stakeholders to vote on the probability and impact of the risk events

37   You have just been assigned as project manager for a large manufacturing project. This one-year project is about halfway done. It involves five different sellers and 20 members of your company on the project team. You want to quickly review where the project now stands. Which of the following reports would be the MOST helpful in finding such information?
      A. Work status
      B. Progress
      C. Forecast
      D. Communications

38   Who is responsible for the stakeholder expectations management in a high-profile, high-risk project?
      A. Project risk assessment officer
      B. Project management office
      C. Project sponsor
      D. Project manager

39   A stakeholder wants to make a change to the work breakdown structure that does NOT affect the time, risk or cost of the project. What is the BEST thing to do?
      A. Tell the stakeholder that this change cannot be done without revising the project management plan
      B. Make the change
      C. Meet with management
      D. Look for other impacts on the project

40   All of the following are parts of the team's stakeholder management effort EXCEPT?
      A. Giving stakeholders extras
      B. Identifying stakeholders
      C. Determining stakeholders' needs
      D. Managing stakeholders' expectations

Answers

1   A   Train, coach, and educate stakeholders in risk principles and processes in order to create shared understanding of principles and processes, and foster engagement in risk management. This is part of Domain 2 and Stakeholder Engagement

2   D   Risk owners are a dedicated part of the risk response planning and the not the risk management planning

3   D   The questions asks 'Which one of the following statements best describes the requirements for developing a probability and impact matrix'. The purpose on developing a probability and impact is for stakeholder contribution which is Option D

4   C   Assessing stakeholder risk tolerance is performed using processes and tools such as interviewing stakeholders and reviewing historical stakeholder behaviours in order to identify project risk thresholds.

5   D   All options are relevant in gauging the interest and possible influence of stakeholders in a project. This refers to the Power/Interest Grid and Influence/Impact Grid samples that are in Stakeholder Analysis as per the PMBOK

6   D   The answer is D as this shows what Stakeholder Management Involves: -
- Stakeholder identification and management techniques
- Project Managers focuses on managing engagement / expectations
- Managing information to / from stakeholders

7   D   Answer D shows three essential qualities: -
A. taking feedback from the stakeholder
b) using a structured process to manage information and
c) ensuring that the relevant document is updated
All of the above are MUST's when dealing with changing requirements and stakeholders. The other options give some but not all three characteristics

8   D   Identifying stakeholder risk attitudes and cognitive biases is done using stakeholder analysis techniques. This is performed in order to manage stakeholder expectations and responses throughout the life of the project. This is part of Domain 2 (Stakeholder Engagement) Task 5

9   C   The questions is focusing on the unknowns that may be part of the quantitative analysis. The best way of understanding and profiling these for Jon is through Monte Carlo analysis to understand the variations

10 B Assess the engagement level of stakeholders under the headings of: -
- Unaware of the project and impact
- Resistant is aware of the project but resistant to change
- Neutral and is neither supportive nor resistant
- Supportive of change
- Leading and is actively engaging

11 A If you know the tolerances of the stakeholders, you can determine how they might react to different situations and risk events. You use this information to help assign levels of risk on each work package or activity.

12 D With professional responsibility, you must be open and honest with all deliberations. The correct option here is to tell the supplier the situation and agreed a mutually beneficial solution but that is not present, hence you must go with the options that sides on open and honesty and this is choice D

13 D Risk responses reflect an organisation's perceived balance between risk taking and risk avoidance. The other choices are incorrect. Risks need not be induced only external to the project. For example, adopting a fast track schedule may be a conscious choice and result in some risks. This may however be in balance with the reward gained by taking the risk. Risks need not always be negative in nature. They may be positive as well. All projects need to plan for Risks.

14 A A high-level risk register contains the identified risks only. The risk register is created during the Identify Risks process.

15 C The project manager is using a good process, however he/she should have involved the other stakeholders to help identify risks

16 A The risk register contains details of the identified risks

17 D This is one of the trickier test questions. Options B and C are obviously wrong as project stakeholders cannot simply be left out of a meeting just because they reside in another geography. Option A is not optimal because tele-conferencing is less effective than video conferencing. Also, you send meeting notes after a meeting and not during it.

18 C Even though both parties agreed on a set of notes developed by party A, the fact that it was signed by both parties means that it was / is a contract. Hence party B is correct based off the fact that the contract stipulates the work (and only the work) to be done.

19 A Option A is the only option present that would determine why the work should be done by the company itself. All the other options are reasons why the work would be contracted out

20 C While all actions are appropriate, the key to this questions is the word NEXT. The next action the project manager should take on is to meet with the customer and formalise the requirement changes with them as this is their primary responsibility.

21 C The Delphi technique utilises anonymous participation from stakeholders to IDENITY and evaluate ALL (and not just important) risk information.

22 A This is a case of where you are socially responsible and must work with all external entities

23 B As you are preparing the risk response plan, the project requires individuals who can assess and understand what the project is about (i.e. team members, functional managers who are part of stakeholders, senior management, etc.). The sponsor will have the least connection with such information

24 A A project provides risk-related recommendations to stakeholders regarding risk strategy and planning, risk process facilitation, risk reporting, and specialised risk tasks by using effective communication techniques in order to support effective risk-based decision making. This is Domain 2 (Task 7)

25 A When there's a dispute between a buyer and a seller, that's called a claim. Most contracts have some language that explains exactly how claims should be resolved - and since it's in the contract, it's legally binding, and both the buyer and seller need to follow it. Usually it's not an option to renegotiate a contract, especially at the end of the project after the work is complete, and lawsuits should only be filed if there are absolutely, positively no other options

26 A The answers will not be Option C and D. The questions asked ' You want to identify the project stakeholders that will have the most power in relation to their interest on your project'. Based on this, it is a Power / Interest grid which is Option A

27 D The time and money costs required to eliminate the chance of failure is in proportion to the stakeholders' tolerance of risk on the project.

28 B As project manager, you are responsible for including ALL stakeholders into the project. Not until this is done should any situation be escalated. Hence choice B is the NEXT BEST option

29 C When you read this question and in the 'mode' of the exam, then there is only one answer and it is about always following the process

30 A Firstly a control chart is a way of monitoring data trends in projects. The trend is showing a problem and the project manager should investigate by doing a root-cause analysis. This is Option A

31 B At no time should the conditions of the contract be violated without a change order or official claim procedure. The BEST choice is B

32   D   The report is now due and you have a responsibility to report this information to your manager, given that you must report the information to you manager in an open and honest manner and THEN work with the team members to understand why. The correct answer to this question comes back to meeting the objective of the question

33   A   Positive stakeholders are those who would normally benefit from a successful outcome from the project, while negative stakeholders are those who see negative outcomes from the project's success. Negative stakeholders are often overlooked by the project team at the risk of failing to bring the projects to a successful end.

34   C   Anonymous participation will always use the Delphi technique

35   D   Shelly needs to understand risk tolerance and ensure stakeholders are involved in defining probability and impact for the project. This is actually what risk management planning attempts to do and the best option for Shelly to remove these biases is Option D

36   A   The key part of removing bias is for the stakeholder to contribute to the definition of probability and impact. This is step in the risk management planning process and is about understanding stakeholders views and tolerances

37   B   It is either A or B. Work status is about detailed work-package information whereas progress is using Earned Value indices and variances to represent the status. To quickly review where the project now stands, it is better to go with B

38   D   This should be a very straightforward question and the role here is the project manager

39   D   Even though it may not directly affect the time or cost to the project you need to look at all the impacts of a change on other components of the triple constraint (scope, time and quality). The change may increase risk or reduce quality etc.

40   A   Giving stakeholder extra's is gold plating and is not effective

Domain 3: - Risk Process Facilitation Exam

Answer Sheet

Question	Answer	Correction	Question	Answer	Correction
1			21		
2			22		
3			23		
4			24		
5			25		
6			26		
7			27		
8			28		
9			29		
10			30		
11			31		
12			32		
13			33		
14			34		
15			35		
16			36		
17			37		
18			38		
19			39		
20			40		

Exam

1   Will should a project do risk identification?

A. To enable the project team and stakeholders to understand the risk impact of the project.

B. To enable the project team and stakeholders to understand the risk exposure of the project.

C. To enable the project team and stakeholders to analyse the risk exposure of the project.

D. To enable the project team and stakeholders to analyse the risk impact of the project.

2   You are the project manager of the YHG project for your company. Within the project, you and the project team have identified a risk event that could have a schedule impact on the project of 2 months. This risk event has a 70% chance of occurring in the project. The project identifies a solution that will reduce the probability of the risk event to ten percent, but is difficult to implement. Management will not agree on the solution. What should you do in this situation?

A. You should pursue an avoidance strategy.

B. You should pursue a transference strategy.

C. You should identify a contingency plan while continue to pursue a mitigation strategy

D. You should identify a contingency plan

3   You are carrying out a project by outsourcing, and planning to complete it 6 months later. Recently, you find the subcontractor has many troubles between labourers and management, which have caused some of the employees to leave. Luckily enough, the situation has not causing any impact to your project. But as a project manager, which of the following would you do in this situation?

A. Report it to the supervisors and discuss future contingency measures with them.

B. Put pressure on the subcontractor, ensuring he/she will complete your project on planned date.

C. Ask the organisation to replace this subcontractor.

D. Sign an outsourcing contract with the employees performing the project, so as to assure the project will be completed as planned.

4	You are the project manager of the YHG project for your company. Within the project, you and the project team have identified a risk event that could have a financial impact on the project of $450,000. This risk event has a 70 percent chance of occurring in the project. The project identifies a solution that will reduce the probability of the risk event to ten percent, but it will cost $260,000 to implement. Management agrees with the solution and asks that you include the risk response in the project plan. What risk response is this?
A. This is mitigation because the response reduces the probability.
B. This is not a risk response, but a change request.
C. This is transference because of the $260,000 cost of the solution.
D. This is avoidance because the risk response caused the project plan to be changed.

5	Lisa is the project manager of the FKN project for her organisation. She is working with Sam, the CIO, to discuss a discount the vendor has offered the project based on the amount of materials that is ordered. Lisa and Sam review the offer and agree that while their project may qualify for the discounted materials the savings is nominal and they would not necessarily pursue the savings. Lisa documents this positive risk response in the risk register. What risk response is this?
A. Enhance
B. Transference
C. Share
D. Acceptance

6	You are the project manager of the NGH project for your organisation. You want to create a cause and- effect diagram to help discover the root causes of the risks within the project. Harold, the CIO, recommends that you create an Ishikawa diagram instead. What is an Ishikawa diagram?
A. It is a graphical representation of situations showing causal influences.
B. It is the same thing as a root cause diagram.
C. It shows how various elements of a system interrelate.
D. It diagrams the risks according to the work breakdown structure including resources.

7   Your company has won a prestigious project which deals with building software to be used on spaceships landing on the moon. After building the schedule network diagram - you identify the critical path and also a number of Near-Critical Paths. What does this mean with respect to Risks related to Project Schedule?
A. The project is at high risk of meeting its schedule considering additional near critical paths
B. The project has no risks of meeting its schedule considering additional near critical paths
C. Near Critical Path will have no impact on the schedule - hence no risks at all
D. The Near Critical Path activities have a lot of Float - so there is no fear of not meeting the project completion.

8   A risk manager had just been hired to take over risk management responsibilities for a company producing a new pharmaceutical drug for diabetics. During the first cycle of risk identification, it was determined that the project had a high level of risk, and an expert was needed. The risk manager's first order of business is to look over the risk management plan. All of the following are most likely to be addressed within the plan EXCEPT:
A. Stakeholder risk tolerances
B. Budget for risk activities
C. Definitions of risk probability and impact
D. Risk owner

9   Kelly is the project manager of the BHH project for her organisation. She is completing the risk identification process for this portion of her project. Which one of the following is the only thing that the risk identification process will create for Kelly?
A. Risk register
B. Risk register updates
C. Change requests
D. Project document updates

10 You are the project manager of a new project in your organisation. You and the project team have identified the project risks, completed risk analysis, and are planning the most appropriate risk responses. Which of the following tools is most effective to choose the most appropriate risk response?
A. Cause-and-effect diagrams
B. Project network diagrams
C. Delphi Technique
D. Decision tree analysis

11 A part of a project deals with the hardware work. As a project manager, you have decided to hire a company to deal with all hardware work on the project. Which type of risk response is this?
A. Exploit
B. Mitigation
C. Transference
D. Avoidance

12 During the execution of a project, a risk is identified by a team member. This newly identified risk is currently not in the Risk Register. As a Project Manager, what is the first action you would take after being notified of the risk?
A. Discuss the risk with the team to ascertain the impact and probability of the risk
B. Analyse the risk.
C. Hold a meeting with the team leads to determine dependency and secondary risks.
D. Update the Risk Register.

13 A large telecommunications project is about halfway through when you are assigned as the project manager. The project involves three different sellers and a project team of 30 people. You would like to see the project communication requirements and the technology used for communication, where are you likely to find this information?
A. Project information distribution plan
B. The project schedule
C. The stakeholder register
D. The project management plan

14 You are the project manager of QSL project for your organisation. You are working with your project team and several key stakeholders to create a diagram that shows how various elements of a system interrelate and the mechanism of causation within the system. What diagramming technique are you using as a part of the risk identification process?
A. Predecessor and successor diagramming
B. System or process flowcharts
C. Cause and effect diagrams
D. Influence diagrams

15 A Fire Fighter falls in the category of:
A. Risk Ignorant
B. Risk Averse
C. Risk Seeker
D. Risk Neutral

16   There are five outputs of the risk monitoring and controlling process. Which one of the
      following is NOT an output of the process?
      A. Organisational process assets updates
      B. Risk register updates
      C. Vendor contracts
      D. Change requests

17   Which of the following processes has the Risk Register as the primary output?
      A. Perform Qualitative Risk Analysis
      B. Monitor and Control Risks
      C. Plan Risk Management
      D. Identify Risk

18   The purpose of risk status meeting is to:
      A. Exchange information about the project
      B. Have team members report on what they are doing
      C. Issue work authorisations
      D. Confirm the accuracy of the costs submitted by the team

19   As a practicing project manager, you have a responsibility to all of the following
      except:
      A. Satisfy the scope and objectives of your organisation
      B. Provide accurate and truthful representations in the preparation of estimates
      regarding costs, services and expected results
      C. Ensure that each project has a fully developed project charter
      D. Respect the confidentiality of stakeholder

20   Which of the following Tools and Techniques are part of Risk Management Planning?
      A. Risk planning meetings.
      B. Documentation reviews.
      C. Data precision rankings.
      D. Diagramming techniques.

21   You are the project manager of the GYH project for your organisation. Management
      has asked you to begin identifying risks and to use an information gathering technique.
      Which one of the following risk identification approaches is an information gathering
      technique?
      A. Root cause analysis
      B. Assumptions analysis
      C. SWOT analysis
      D. Documentation reviews

22   Beta is the Project Manager of a Road construction project. During a project review, Beta realises that one particular risk has occurred. To take appropriate action against risk that has happened, Beta needs to refer to which document?
A. Risk response plan
B. Risk management plan
C. Risk breakdown structure
D. Risk register

23   During which stage of Risk planning are risks prioritised based on probability and impact?
A. Identify Risks
B. Plan Risk responses
C. Perform Qualitative risk analysis
D. Perform Quantitative risk analysis

24   A project manager asked various stakeholders to determine the probability and impact of a number of risks. He then analysed assumptions. He is about to move to the next step of risk management. Based on this information, what has the project manager forgotten to do?
A. Evaluate trends in risk analysis.
B. Identify triggers.
C. Provide a standardised risk rating matrix.
D. Create a fallback plan.

25   During which stage of Risk planning are modelling techniques used to determine overall effects of risks on project objectives for high probability, high impact risks?
A. Identify Risks
B. Plan Risk responses
C. Perform Qualitative risk analysis
D. Perform Quantitative risk analysis

26   What should project contingency reserve be evaluated on?
A. The risk exposure of the project
B. The risk impact of the project
C. The risk probability of the project
D. The risk tolerance of the project

27   Which of the following processes has risk register as the primary output?
A. Plan Risk Management
B. Identify Risks
C. Monitoring and Control Risks
D. Perform Qualitative Risk Analysis

28 Techniques such as force field analysis, scenario planning, futures thinking, visualisation, Delphi groups and nominal group technique are associated with which risk management area:
A. Risk Planning
B. Risk Identification
C. Qualitative Risk Analysis
D. Quantitative Risk Analysis

29 Which of the following risk management processes numerically analyses the effects of identified risks on the project objectives?
A. Identify Risks
B. Perform Qualitative Risk Analysis
C. Perform Quantitative Risk Analysis
D. Plan Risk Responses

30 In which process of Project Risk Management knowledge area are numeric values assigned to probabilities and impact of risks
A. Perform Qualitative Risk Analysis
B. Perform Quantitative Risk Analysis
C. Perform Numeric Risk Analysis
D. Plan Risk Response

31 Your company has bagged a number of government contracts dealing with setting up infrastructure. This includes setting up roads and bridges. This is a very big and prestigious project so your company would like to ensure everything is planned well in advance. You are the project manager of this project. Considering its importance - you and your team come up with a list of risks. One of the subject matter experts indicates that during the months of July and August the construction work of the bridge across the river would need to stop on account of past history of flooding of the river. You agree with the expert and plan the schedule accordingly. What strategy did you just apply?
A. Accept
B. Exploit
C. Mitigate
D. Transfer

32 During which stage of risk planning are risks prioritised based on their relative probability and impact?
A. Identify Risks
B. Perform Qualitative risk analysis
C. Perform Quantitative risk analysis
D. Plan Risk Responses

33   Techniques such as integrated cost/schedule analysis is associated with which risk
      management area:
      A. Risk Monitor and Control
      B. Risk Identification
      C. Qualitative Risk Analysis
      D. Quantitative Risk Analysis

34   What are workarounds in project management?
      A. Workarounds are essentially the same as rework.
      B. Workarounds are alternative strategies.
      C. Workarounds are unplanned responses to emerging risks that were previously
      unidentified or accepted.
      D. Workarounds are activities performed according to applicable contingency plans

35   A project has just lost its priority from being one of the key projects that the
      organisation was interested in to one of a low priority. This introduces risk belonging to
      which category?
      A. Organisational
      B. Technical
      C. Environmental
      D. External

36   You work as a project manager for BlueWell Inc. You are working with your team
      members on the risk responses in the project. Which risk response will likely cause a
      project to use the procurement processes?
      A. Exploiting
      B. Mitigation
      C. Sharing
      D. Acceptance

37   Risk Management is designed to increase the likelihood of positive events vs the
      likelihood and impact of negative events affecting a project. There are several
      processes recommended for identifying and tackling risks. Which of the following
      processes occurs first?
      A. Qualitative risk analysis
      B. Planning risk responses
      C. Quantitative risk analysis
      D. Identifying risks

38 You work as a project manager for BlueWell Inc. You have to communicate the causes of risk events to the stakeholders. Which risk diagramming technique you will use to communicate the causes of risk events to project stakeholders?
A. Project network diagrams
B. Process flow charts
C. Ishikawa diagrams
D. Influence diagrams

39 You were in the middle of a two-year project to deploy new technology to field offices across the country. A hurricane caused power outages just when the upgrade was near completion. When the power was restored, all of the project reports and historical data were lost with no way of retrieving them. What should have been done to prevent this problem?
A. Purchase insurance.
B. Plan for a reserve fund.
C. Monitor the weather and have a contingency plan.
D. Schedule the installation outside of the hurricane season.

40 All of the following are inputs of the Identify Risks process EXCEPT:
A. Organisational process assets
B. Enterprise environmental factors
C. Project charter
D. Project documents

nswers

1　B　Risk identification is performed in order to enable the project team and stakeholders to understand and determine the risk exposure of the project. This is Domain 3 (Task 2). Both Option C and D are risk analysis tasks

2　A　This is a difficult question to answer. The key to this question is that management have not agreed to the strategy and no reason as to why is given. The project manager in this instance must prepare and protect the project (which is the contingency plan) and continue to implement a mitigation strategy for the risk. This is the best option for the project and hence Option C is correct

3　A　The open and honest legal consideration is choice A. All others are not dealing with the situation at hand and are professionally unethical

4　A　When you read this line 'The project identifies a solution that will reduce the probability of the risk event to ten percent, but it will cost $260,000 to implement', it should immediately mean mitigation. This risk probability is been reduced

5　D　Since they are not pursuing the saving, this is consider to be acceptance. The risk is an opportunity so the outcome of the risk is positive

6　B　This should be a simple enough question and it is asking what an Ishikawa diagram is. This is a cause and effect diagram

7　A　The correct answer is A - greater the number of near critical paths greater the risk of the project not meeting its scheduled completion dates. This is because the Near Critical Path activities will have very little float - so thereby hardly any flexibility - so any slippages in these tasks - in addition to tasks on the Critical Path can lead to schedule slippage. This is why Options B, C and D are incorrect.

8　D　The risk owner is a part of the risk response process and not part of the risk management plan

9　A　Both Option C and D are not correct as they are not relevant for the risk management process. The question asks "Which one of the following is the only thing that the risk identification process will create for Kelly" ... the only option which is valid is A as this is identified as part of the risk deification process

10　D　A decision tree is used to understand the options that are associated with a particular strategy. If you read the question, it states 'You and the project team have identified the project risks, completed risk analysis, and are planning the most appropriate risk responses. Which of the following tools is most effective to choose the most appropriate risk response'. In this case all the qualitative analysis is done and the next thing to do is the quantitative analysis (Option D)

11　C　This should be a straight forward questions and requires you to understand the various risk response strategies. This is an example of transference

12 B When the Project Manager is notified of a risk, it is her responsibility to analyse the risk and take it further. She can ask for more details from the team, if required. However, the first action will always be to analyse the risk.

13 D Option D is the only referred to plan that covers communication. Such a plan is integrates the communication management plan which is a better answer for this.

14 B When you read the line 'You are working with your project team and several key stakeholders to create a diagram that shows how various elements of a system interrelate and the mechanism of causation within the system', the focus here is on the systems and what causes the system to operate. This is a system process flowcharting technique

15 C The correct answer is "Risk Seeker"

16 C This is a typical RMP question and if focused on your understanding of the logic of risk management. Option A, B and D are considered all to be inputs to risk management monitoring and C is an output

17 D The process of Identify Risks has the Risk Register as the major output.

18 A The primary purpose of a status meeting to exchange information. It is certainly facilitated by team members reporting on what they are doing (choice B) but the PRIMARY purpose is Choice A

19 C You can argue that all options are the responsibility of the project manager, however option C is the responsibility of the performing organisation / senior manager and hence option C is the correct answer.

20 A In order to perform risk management planning, meeting are required with the relevant stakeholders

21 A All of the answers are risk identification tools but only one is a diagramming technique considered to be for data gathering. This is Option A

22 A Beta needs to refer to the Risk response plan that documents responses to identified risks

23 C Risk probability and impact are defined during Qualitative risk analysis

24 C The activities of qualitative risk analysis are probability and impact definition, assumptions testing and probability and impact matrix development.

25 D Modelling techniques used to determine overall effects of risks on project objectives for high probability, high impact risks are used during the quantitative stage of the risk process

26 A Project contingency reserve based on the risk exposure of the project in order to have the capability and resources to respond to realised risks.

27 B Process of Identify Risks has Risk register as the major output.

28 B Advanced risk identification tools and techniques for both threats and opportunities (including but not limited to force field analysis, scenario planning, futures thinking, visualisation, Delphi groups, and nominal group technique)

29 C Numerical analysis is associated with Perform Quantitative Risk Analysis

30 B A numeric value is assigned to risks impact and probability during the Quantitative Risk Analysis process.

31 A This is an example of Risk acceptance strategy as there is nothing you can do about situations not in our control. Exploit is meant for positive situations while risk mitigation is where you have a strategy to either reduce the risk impact or probability. Neither is transfer correct as the question does not state that someone else will be responsible for handling the risk.

32 B Perform Qualitative Risk Analysis assesses the impact and likelihood of identified risks. During this process the risks are prioritised based on their relative probability and impact

33 D Advanced quantitative risk analysis tools and techniques includes but are not limited to, integrated cost/schedule analysis, advanced Monte Carlo analysis, system dynamics, bowtie analysis, analytical hierarchy process, risk-based earned value analysis, risk-based critical chain analysis, and multi-factor regression analysis, modelling techniques, advanced risk metric analysis [including statistical process control])

34 C Choice C is the best answer as a workaround is a plan for emerging risks which are not planned for or happen to appear when leas expected

35 A The scenario refers to project prioritisation through a portfolio management review. This is an example of organisational risk

36 C Sharing is a positive risk response which is related to transference. Sharing is the response strategy that invokes a procurement related strategy

37 D Identifying risks is the process of determining which risks may affect a project and documenting their characteristics.

38 C This is a simple question from the exam and it focuses on your knowledge of tools and techniques. A cause and effect diagram can also be called a fishbone or Ishikawa diagram

39 C This is a typical case of be proactive rather than reactive. While the probability of a hurricane is slight and you may argue that this is a once in a million occurrence, the question asks what should have been done to prevent the problem, the answer in this case is to be proactive and monitor the situation with a back-up / workaround plan in place if needed (option C)

40   D   This is a standard inputs / output question. Be careful in reading the question, it states the inputs to 'Identify Risks' which will include: -
- Organisational process assets: - Past project experiences that can influence the current project
- Enterprise environmental factors: - External factors to the project that can influence the current project
- Project charter: - This is the initiation document that can be used to identify risk
The exception here is Option D as that can be considered as an output (i.e. the risk register is a project document)

Domain 4: - Risk Monitoring and Control Exam

Answer Sheet

Question	Answer	Correction	Question	Answer	Correction
1			21		
2			22		
3			23		
4			24		
5			25		
6			26		
7			27		
8			28		
9			29		
10			30		
11			31		
12			32		
13			33		
14			34		
15			35		
16			36		
17			37		
18			38		
19			39		
20			40		

Exam

1   Which of the following should be used to communicate risk management activities and status?
   A. Standard and custom reports using risk registers
   B. Standard and custom reports using risk-related analysis
   C. Standard and custom reports using risk-related metrics
   D. Standard and custom reports using earned value metrics

2   Purchasing insurance is BEST considered an example of risk:
   A. Mitigation.
   B. Transfer.
   C. Acceptance.
   D. Avoidance

3   In what portion of a project are risk and opportunities greatest and require intense planning and anticipation of risk events?
   A. Closing
   B. Planning
   C. Initiating
   D. Executing

4   What should be done with risks on the watch list?
   A. Document them for historical use on other projects.
   B. Document them and revisit during project executing.
   C. Document them and set them aside because they are already covered in your contingency plans.
   D. Document them and give them to the customer.

5   After conducting a SWOT Analysis, you have determined that a business deal is worth pursuing. You are required to use Agile development practices. In your company, there is no expertise in Agile development. Hence, you partner with another organisation that specialises in Agile development. This is an example of:
   A. Sharing a Positive Risk
   B. Mitigating a Negative Risk
   C. Exploiting a Positive Risk
   D. Accepting a Negative Risk

6   Don has hired Jerry, a contractor, to complete a portion of his project work. The contract used was a cost-plus contract. If Don were to perform a risk audit, who would carry the risk in this scenario?
   A. Don would because he is the project manager.
   B. Jerry would because of the contract type.
   C. Don would because of the contract type.
   D. Jerry would because he is the hired contractor.

7   You work as a project manager for BlueWell Inc. You are working with Nancy, the COO of your company, on several risks within the project. Nancy understands that through qualitative analysis you have identified 80 risks that have a low probability and low impact as the project is currently planned. Nancy's concern, however, is that the impact and probability of these risk events may change as conditions within the project may change. She would like to know where will you document and record these 80 risks that have low probability and low impact for future reference. What should you tell Nancy?
A. Risks with low probability and low impact are recorded in a watchlist for future monitoring.
B. All risks, regardless of their assessed impact and probability, are recorded in the risk log.
C. Risk identification is an iterative process so any changes to the low probability and low impact risks will be reassessed throughout the project life cycle.
D. All risks are recorded in the risk management plan.

8   You work as a project manager for BlueWell Inc. Your project is using a new material to construct a large warehouse in your city. This new material is cheaper than traditional building materials, but it takes some time to learn how to use the material properly. You have communicated to the project stakeholders that you will be able to save costs by using the new material, but you will need a few extra weeks to complete training to use the materials. This risk response of learning how to use the new materials can also be known as what term?
A. Team development
B. Benchmarking
C. Cost of conformance to quality
D. Cost-benefits analysis

9   Which of the following processes involves choosing the alternative strategies, executing a contingency or fallback plan, taking corrective action, and modifying the project management plan?
A. Monitor and Control risk
B. Configuration Management
C. Perform Risk Response
D. Risk Identification

10   Workarounds are determined during which risk management process?
A. Risk identification
B. Quantitative risk analysis
C. Risk response planning
D. Risk monitoring and control

11   Bill is the project manager for a project that will last six months and has a budget of $580,000. In this project a high-risk has been identified with the new materials the project will be using. Bill would like to assign one person, Beth, to be responsible to monitor this risk. Bill assigns Beth the authority to respond to the risk event if it appears in the risk events that is likely to happen. In addition, Bill hires a consultant to work with Beth on this area of the project. In this instance, who is the risk response owner?

    A. Bill, because he is the project manager

    B. Beth, because she has the authority to respond to the risk event

    C. Beth and the consultant are the risk owners

    D. The consultant working with Beth, because this is transference

12   Ted is the project manager of the HRR project for his company. Management has asked that Ted periodically reviews the contingency reserve as risk events happen, pass, or are still pending. What is the purpose of reviewing the contingency reserve?

    A. It helps to evaluate if the remaining reserve is adequate for the risk exposure.

    B. It helps to determine how much more funds will need to be invested in the project.

    C. It helps to evaluate secondary and residual risks related to the risk responses and their costs.

    D. It helps to determine the probability and impact of project risks.

13   You are the project manager of the GHY project for your company. This project has a budget of $543,000 and is expected to last 18 months. In this project, you have identified several risk events and created risk response plans. In what project management process group will you implement risk response plans?

    A. Executing

    B. Planning

    C. Monitoring and Controlling

    D. In any process group where the risk event resides

14   Tracy is the project manager of the NLT Project for her company. The NLT Project is scheduled to last 14 months and has a budget at completion of $4,555,000. Tracy's organisation will receive a bonus of $80,000 per day that the project is completed early up to $800,000. Tracy realises that there are several opportunities within the project to save on time by crashing the project work. Crashing the project is what type of risk response?

    A. Transference

    B. Mitigation

    C. Exploit

    D. Enhance

15   Mathew is a Project Manager for software migration at a bank. A major risk that has
      been identified is attrition of resources. As a strategy to respond to this risk, Mathew,
      with support from Senior Management, provides good increments to his team
      members. What type of risk response is Mathew following?
      A. Accept
      B. Avoid
      C. Transfer
      D. Mitigate

16   Which of these is not a valid response to positive risks?
      A. Exploit
      B. Mitigate
      C. Enhance
      D. Share

17   Which of the following processes must be repeated after Plan Risk Responses, as well
      as part of the Monitor and Control Risks, to determine if the overall project risk has
      been satisfactorily decreased?
      A. Risk Limitation
      B. Perform Qualitative Risk Analysis
      C. Identify Risk
      D. Perform Quantitative Risk Analysis

18   Which of the following processes is described in the statement below? "This is the
      process of numerically analysing the effect of identified risks on overall project
      objectives."
      A. Identify Risks
      B. Perform Quantitative Risk Analysis
      C. Monitor and Control Risks
      D. Perform Qualitative Risk Analysis

19   How are risk lessons learnt captured?
      A. Through comprehensive review of the project risk management plan, risk register,
      risk audits, earned value data and other associated reports.
      B. Through comprehensive review of the project risk management plan, risk register,
      risk audits, risk process performance reports and other associated reports.
      C. Through comprehensive review of the project risk management plan, risk register,
      risk audits, risk register performance and other associated reports.
      D. Through comprehensive review of the project communication management plan,
      risk register, risk reviews, risk process metrics and other associated reports.

20 Which of the following risk response strategies involves outsourcing the risky projects?
A. Mitigate
B. Exploit
C. Share
D. Transfer

21 Your company has won a large project for one of the fund houses to administer their funds. The project work has been going on smoothly and the customer has been singing praises about the work done so far. The client has planned a visit the next month to go over the plans for the next phase of the project as well as to meet with the project team. Your senior management realises that this client could potentially need additional capabilities in the derivatives segment. Your company happens to have a strong exposure to this segment having executed numerous such projects. Your senior manager also invites key managers from the derivatives segment to showcase the organisations abilities in the derivatives vertical - this is an example of?
A. Mitigating the risk
B. Avoiding the risk
C. Transferring the risk
D. Exploiting the risk

22 You work as a project manager for BlueWell Inc. You would like to utilise sensitivity analysis in your project, but the management does not understand how this will be displayed. What type of chart is usually used with sensitivity analysis to show the relative affect of risks on the project?
A. Ishikawa chart
B. Force field analysis chart
C. GERT Chart
D. Tornado diagram

23 Ruth is the project manager of ISFH project for her company. This project is forty percent complete and it appears that some risk events are going to happen in the project that will have an adverse affect on the project. Ruth creates a change request regarding the risks. Is this a valid response?
A. No, change requests should not address risks, only risk response strategies should be issued.
B. No, change requests should not address pending risks, but only scope changes.
C. Yes, change requests can be recommended for corrective actions for contingency plans.
D. Yes, change requests can ask for additional funds to pay for the risk impact.

24   Your team has just bagged a software development project. The executive
      management is very pleased as this is a very prestigious project. However you are a
      little worried considering the complex nature of the project. You decide to try and
      identify the possible risks. You get all relevant stakeholders together and conduct
      mammoth discussions. Together you have come up with a number of risks. However
      based on your experience - you still feel that not all the risks have been identified. You
      decide to set aside some budget for the risks that you have not identified but are sure
      you will encounter. Where does this budget come from?
      A. Cost Management Plan
      B. Cost Baseline
      C. Contingency Reserves
      D. Management Reserve

25   Which of the following tools and techniques are used to support risk decision making?
      A. Assumption Analysis
      B. Prioritisation
      C. Delphi Technique
      D. Risk Breakdown Structures

26   Lisa is the project manager of the SQL project for her company. She has completed
      the risk response planning with her project team and is now ready to update the risk
      register to reflect the risk response. Which of the following statements best describes
      the level of detail Lisa should include with the risk responses she has created?
      A. The level of detail is set by historical information.
      B. The level of detail should correspond with the priority ranking.
      C. The level of detail must define exactly the risk response for each identified risk.
      D. The level of detail is set of project risk governance.

27   All of the following statements are true, EXCEPT:
      A. Risk management is a proactive approach to project management.
      B. Risk management should begin with a thorough and realistic review of the project.
      C. Risk management begins early on in the project, when information is minimal.
      D. Risk management begins early on in the project, as soon as the project scope is
      defined.

28   A project manager of Cyber Channels Inc. is in the process of identifying project risks.
      While reviewing how the elements of a particular system interrelate, she discovers two
      risks relating to the cause of another risk that were both initially overlooked. Which of
      the following techniques is the project manager using?
      A. Influence diagram
      B. Flow chart
      C. Cause and effect diagram
      D. Control charts

29   A system development project is nearing project closing when a previously unidentified risk is discovered. This could potentially affect the project's overall ability to deliver. What should be done NEXT?
A. Alert the project sponsor of potential impacts to cost, scope, or schedule.
B. Qualify the risk.
C. Mitigate this risk by developing a risk response plan.
D. Develop a workaround.

30   An output of risk response planning is:
A. Residual risks.
B. Risks identified.
C. Prioritised list of risks.
D. Impacts identified.

31   While preparing your risk responses, you identify additional risks. What should you do?
A. Add reserves to the project to accommodate the new risks and notify management.
B. Document the risk items, and calculate the expected monetary value based on probability and impact that result from the occurrences.
C. Determine the risk events and the associated cost, then add the cost to the project budget as a reserve.
D. Add a 10 percentage contingency to the project budget and notify the customer.

32   What should be used to drive risk process improvements?
A. Analysis of risk process performance against established metrics
B. Analysis of risk register information
C. Analysis of risk analysis data against process measurements
D. Analysis of decision tree options and expected monetary values

33   There are four inputs to the Monitoring and Controlling Project Risks process. Which one of the following will NOT help you, the project manager, to prepare for risk monitoring and controlling?
A. Work Performance Information
B. Project management plan
C. Risk register
D. Change requests

34   During a post-mortem meeting, discussion arises about who has to take responsibility for some major failures. It has become obvious that the attendees of the meeting will not come to a jointly accepted conclusion. What is not an appropriate strategy for such a situation?
A. Separate the people from the problem
B. Focus on interests, not positions
C. Insist on objective criteria and standards
D. Suspend the discussion and schedule another meeting

35 A reserve is generally intended to be used for: -
A. Rework activities
B. Compensate for inaccurate project estimates
C. Reducing the risk of missing the cost or schedule objectives
D. Compensate for inaccurate project schedule estimates

36 A project manager of a retail chain of hardware stores is in the process of conducting risk identification activities. Along with the risk management team, the project manager examined the existing project plans to determine whether they were consistent with the project requirements. What technique is the project manager currently using?
A. Process flow chart
B. Checklist analysis
C. Brainstorming
D. Documentation reviews

37 You work as a project manager for BlueWell Inc. You with your team are using a method or a (technical) process that conceives the risks even if all theoretically possible safety measures would be applied. One of your team member wants to know what a residual risk is. What will you reply to your team member?
A. It is a risk that cannot be addressed by a risk response.
B. It is a risk that will remain no matter what type of risk response is offered.
C. It is a risk that remains because no risk response is taken.
D. It is a risk that remains after planned risk responses are taken.

38 A vendor left you a voicemail saying your equipment will not be arriving on time. You identified a risk response for this risk and have arranged for a local company to lease you the needed equipment until yours arrives. This is an example of which risk response strategy?
A. Transference
B. Acceptance
C. Mitigation
D. Avoidance

39 Which of the following statements is true regarding the issue logs?
A. Issue logs describe the ground rules and conflict management procedures to manage the project
B. Issue logs are written logs that address the roles and responsibilities of each project team member
C. Issue logs are inputs to the Manage Project Team process and outputs of Manage Stakeholder Engagement
D. Issue logs are a graphic display of project team members and their reporting relationships

40   Which positive risk response best describes a teaming agreement?
      A. Share
      B. Exploit
      C. Enhance
      D. Venture

Answers

1	C	Standard and custom reports using risk-related metrics as specified in the risk management plan are used in order to communicate risk management activities and status to stakeholders
2	B	To mitigate risk (choice A. we either reduce the probability of the event happening or reduce its impact. Many people think of using insurance as a way of decreasing impact. However, mitigating risk is taking action before a risk event occurs. Buying insurance is not such an action. Acceptance of risk (choice C) does not involve such action as purchasing insurance. Avoidance of risk (choice D) means we change the way we will execute the project so the risk is no longer a factor. Transference is passing the risk off to another party.
3	C	This is hopefully a simple enough question and the standard answer is initiation as this is where the greatest level of uncertainty resides
4	B	Risk need to be actively managed / monitored by the project. The only answer that alludes to this is answer B. All others are a means of risk response except for A which occurs only on project close-out
5	A	This is an example of responding to an opportunity (positive risk). There are four strategies to respond to positive risks.
6	C	The key to this question is understand the risk associated with contract types: - 1. Fixed prices contracts is where Jerry is accepting the risk 2. Cost price or Cost plus contracts is where the risk is shared but the project can be accepting of the majority of risks 3. Time and Materials (T&M) contracts is where Don is fully accepting the risk. As the contract is cost-plus, Don is accepting of the risk
7	A	Both Option A and Option B are good options. The key part of Option A is that these risks should be monitoring, there does not need to be a proactive action / plan against the low order risks
8	C	This is a generic question and brings some information from the different areas of the PMBOK® Guide. When looking at the question, it is not Option A and B. So this is a choice between C and D and the question does mention saving costs which means that it is answer C
9	A	The key item in this question is taking corrective action and this may lead you away from Option C and select Option A. This is where the project is not executing on the risk response and not developing the risk response
10	D	A workaround refers to determining how to handle a risk that occurs but is not included in the risk register. The project must be in risk monitoring and control if risks have occurred.

11	B	The question asks who is the risk response owner and not the owner of the risk. Beth is dealing with the risk and hence is the risk response owner
12	A	Contingency reserve is an essential part of risk response to understand what reserve / funds are required to deal with the occurrence of the knowns / unknowns (risk). The option that best describes this is Option A
13	C	The question asks which project process group will you IMPLEMENT the risk response plan. The ask has to be Monitor and Control which is Option C
14	D	If you remember from the PMBOK® Guide, Crashing is when you reduce the schedule by increasing resources. However the key to this question is Tracy's thinking, she is trying to increase the opportunity of the project which is a positive risk response (Option C or D) but she is not 100% guaranteed of the opportunity (Option D)
15	D	Mathew is mitigating the risk by reducing the probability of risk happening
16	B	Risk mitigation is a response to negative risks and not positive risks. Positive risks may be responded by - "Exploit", "Enhance", "Share", "Accept"
17	D	The question is asking which area of analysis should be performed to understand if the overall project risk is decreased. This is the function of quantitative analysis as this is where the risk exposure is understood. The function of qualitative analysis is to understand the prioritised risks.
18	B	The objective of quantitative analysis is to understand the numeric impact that a risk or risks have on the project objective. This is Option B. the objective of qualitative analysis is to understand the list of risks that can impact the project
19	C	Capture risk lessons learned through comprehensive review of the project risk management plan, risk register, risk audits, risk process performance reports, and other associated reports in order to incorporate into future risk planning.
20	D	This is a case of transferring
21	D	This is an example of exploiting the risk. As the question states the client is happy with the work progress and also there might be an opportunity that the client might be interested in the derivatives segment. So this is an opportunity that could lead to more business. By inviting key managers from the other segment - you are enhancing the possibility of generating additional revenue - so this is an example of exploiting the risk. Note that this is a positive risk.
22	D	The question asks, what type of chart is usually used with sensitivity analysis to show the relative effect of risks on the project. There are two common types of charts used, spider diagrams or tornado diagrams.

23   C   The answer to this question is that change orders are valid and welcomed and will be a trigger to draw down / use contingency. If you chose Option D, this option is not linked with the risk allocation and is more to do with cost allocation

24   D   The type of risk here is an unknown risk. For known risks risk responses can be proactively planned for. For the known risks where we cannot plan proactively - we set aside a reserve called Contingency Reserves. For unknown risks we set aside a Management Reserve. Cost management Plan deals with how you will manage costs on your project and Cost baseline is the baselined cost expected to be expended on the project.

25   B   Estimation tools and techniques to support risk decision making (including but not limited to prioritisation, cost-benefit analysis, analogous, parametric, and bottom-up)

26   B   The level of detail of a risk response strategy should always be associated with the level of priority of the risk itself. The higher the priority (from the analysis) should dictate the level of response

27   D   Both Option B and D are valid options to this question. However, the risk management process (i.e. risk identification) should start at the earliest point in the project and not just when the project scope is defined

28   C   This is an example of cause and effect diagrams. You might argue influence diagrams as an answer but they are not interested in cause, but association

29   B   The key word is NEXT; a risk is discovered and the next thing to do is measure it which is the same a qualify the risk (option B). All other option refer to responding to the risk and this should not be done until the risk is assessed

30   A   Risks are identified (choice B) during risk identification and risk monitoring and control. Prioritised risks (choice C) are documented during qualitative and quantitative risk analysis. Impacts (choice D) are generally determined during quantitative risk analysis. The best answer is A.

31   B   The questions poses the situation that you have identified additional risks and what is the next step ... the next step is the evaluation of these risks which can be either qualitative or quantitative. Given this, the best and only option is B

32   A   Analysis of risk process performance against established metrics in order to drive risk process improvements.

33   D   The question asks which one of the following will NOT help you, the project manager, to prepare for risk monitoring and controlling?
- Work Performance Information supplies the progress of information on the project and risk response
- Project management plan presents the baseline to understand / benchmark performance
- Risk register present the risks and the required responses
Change requests (Option D) is the odd one out and comes about as a result of the monitoring and controlling

34   A   This is a situation where the project manager stakeholder management skills are brought into question. The simple solution here is the project manager should identify the problems and not get over-engaged with the people's emotions. Correct option is A

35   C   Reserve is allocated for the unknowns of a project and not for inaccurate estimates. It would be considered that if the estimates are inaccurate they should be worked on during the planning.

36   D   The project manager is examining the current project management plan. This is an example of document reviews which is Option D

37   D   The simple definition for residual risk is that risk remains as the risk response plan is being carried one. Be careful on the difference between residual and secondary (new risk introduce as the risk response plan is being carried out) risk

38   C   You are taking action with excludes acceptance as being the answer (B). The response is not transferring the risk to any other party and this excludes answer A. So the choice is Mitigation or Avoidance; the second company may still incur a delay and hence the risk is still evident so mitigation (answer C) is the correct option. Avoidance is defined as eliminating the risk.

39   C   Choice A is incorrect because issue logs do not describe any rules and procedures to manage a project.
Choice B is incorrect because issue log does not describe roles and responsibilities of project team, this is taken care by the human resource plan.
Choice C is correct. Issue logs are inputs to the Manage Project Team process and outputs of Manage Stakeholder Engagement
Choice D is incorrect as issue logs do not portray project team members and their reporting relationship. This is taken care of in the RAM.

40   A   The three positive risk responses are: -
- Share
- Exploit
- Enhance

Domain 5: - Perform Specialized Risk Activities

Answer Sheet

Question	Answer	Correction	Question	Answer	Correction
1			21		
2			22		
3			23		
4			24		
5			25		
6			26		
7			27		
8			28		
9			29		
10			30		
11			31		
12			32		
13			33		
14			34		
15			35		
16			36		
17			37		
18			38		
19			39		
20			40		

Exam

1   You are a project manager for a project. The project specialises in generating sufficient power for the national grid across the city or across the country. Your project involves upgrading the nationwide network. Your lead engineer has given you the following estimates for a critical path activity: 60 days most likely, 72 days pessimistic, 48 days optimistic. What is the expected value, or weighted average?
    A. 54
    B. 66
    C. 60
    D. 30

2   You are the project manager of the NGH project for your organisation. You want to create a decision tree diagram to help discover the options and relative risk available to the project. Have completed the decision tree which of the following tools could be used to compliment the project analysis?
    A. Work breakdown structures
    B. Root cause diagram.
    C. Qualitative analysis
    D. Monte Carlo analysis

3   All of the following are diagramming techniques, used within the Identify Risks process, EXCEPT:
    A. Herzberg Diagram
    B. Ishikawa Diagram
    C. Fishbone Diagram
    D. Influence Diagram

4   You are the project manager and working on the process of Monitor and Control Risks. Which of the following is NOT Tools and Techniques you can use for this process?
    A. Risk Audits
    B. Variance and Trend Analysis
    C. Sensitivity Analysis
    D. Reserve Analysis

5   You are the project manager of the CUL project in your organisation. You and the project team are assessing the risk events and creating a probability and impact matrix for the identified risks. Which one of the following statements best describes the requirements for the data type used in qualitative risk analysis?
    A. A qualitative risk analysis requires fast and simple data to complete the analysis.
    B. A qualitative risk analysis requires accurate and unbiased data if it is to be credible.
    C. A qualitative risk analysis encourages biased data to reveal risk tolerances.
    D. A qualitative risk analysis required unbiased stakeholders with biased risk tolerances.

5   Mike works as a project manager for BlueWell Inc. He is determining which risks can affect the project. Mike is looking for the process on how cost estimates will be used to qualify risk. Which of the following should Tom use?
A. Activity cost estimates
B. Cost management plan
C. Activity duration estimates
D. Risk management plan

7   Your project has met with an unexpected problem. The supply of a critical component of your final product is delayed by 25 days. You need to show an alpha prototype of the product in 15 days. You've called a brainstorming team meeting to determine if you can deliver this limited version without the critical component. What are you trying to create?
A. A risk management plan
B. A risk mitigation strategy
C. A workaround
D. An updated scope baseline

8   All of the following are tools used for performing variance and trend analysis EXCEPT?
A. Earned value analysis
B. Variance analysis
C. Trend analysis
D. Decision tree analysis

9   If the cost of insurance is $10,000, the value of the property is $100,000, and the probability of loss is ten percent, what is the expected cost of the insurance?
A. The same as the cost of the probable loss and there is no advantage
B. Desirable because it will cost less than the probable losses
C. Undesirable because it costs more than the probable losses
D. None of the above

10   During a status meeting, two project team members began a heated argument that escalated to the point that half the room was involved. The project manager had her hands full in keeping the room under control. What are the team members most likely arguing about?
A. Resources
B. Schedule
C. Cost
D. Priorities

11   The project manager is in the process of evaluating bids on a scope of work that neither the team nor others in the organisation are familiar with. Which of the following would be the best technique to ensure that there are no significant differences in understanding of scope and risk with the prospective seller?
A. Weighting system
B. Screening system
C. Expected value
D. Independent estimate

12   You are a risk auditor for your company. You are reviewing the contract types a project manager has used in her project. Of the following, which contract type has the most risk for the project manager as a buyer?
A. Cost plus percentage of costs
B. Time and material
C. Cost plus incentive fee
D. Fixed-price, incentive fee

13   You are a project manager for product development. Your project involves upgrading the nationwide network for the company. Your lead engineer has given you the following estimates for a critical path activity: 60 days most likely, 72 days pessimistic, 48 days optimistic. What is the standard deviation?
A. 22
B. 20
C. 2
D. 4

14   Andrew is a Project Manager for Green Valley project. A risk management plan has been prepared for the project. Which of the following should Andrew do next?
A. Perform Qualitative risk analysis
B. Perform Quantitative risk analysis
C. Identify Risks
D. Plan Risk responses

15   John Strauss is a Project Manager for a reforestation project. To identify the risks involved, John sends a questionnaire to gather inputs from experts. Which technique is John using?
A. Delphi technique
B. Interviews
C. Brain storming
D. Documentation review

6 Pete works as a project manager for BlueWell Inc. The Management has told him that he must implement an agreed-upon contingency response if the cost performance index in his project is less than 0.90. Consider that Pete's project has a budget at completion of $275,000. His project is 65 percent complete and he has spent $175,000 to date. However, Pete is scheduled to be 78 percent complete. What is the cost performance index for this project to determine if the contingency response should happen?
A. 1.02
B. 0.96
C. 0.90
D. 0.89

7 You are the project manager of the NNQ Project for your company and are working with your project team to define contingency plans for the risks within your project. Mark, one of your project team members, asks what tool and technique should be used to identify contingency what a contingency plan is. Which of the following statements best defines what a contingency response is?
A. Delphi technique
B. Nominal group analysis
C. Monte Carlo analysis
D. Risk response analysis

8 A project manager liked to hold meetings on a weekly basis with his team members. These meetings resembled brainstorming sessions, where ideas were generated regarding existing risks and project issues. The project manager never struck down any idea, and instead, attempted to foster an environment where creativity and sharing of ideas was encouraged. What type of leadership style does this project manager use?
A. Facilitating
B. Directing
C. Consultative
D. Co-Managing

9 You are in charge of a painting project for a high rise building. As part of the planning - you need to take a decision of buy Vs lease for some stilt ladders needed on site. The cost of the ladder is 1000 $ and a daily cost of 4$ while the daily lease cost is 12$.If you were to lease the ladder - what should be the duration to ensure your decision is correct?
A. A duration less than 126 days
B. A duration less than 150 days
C. A duration greater than 126 days
D. A duration greater than 126 days

20 You are preparing to start the qualitative risk analysis process for your project. You will be relying on some organisational process assets to influence the process. Which one of the following is NOT a probable reason for relying on organisational process assets as an input for qualitative risk analysis?
A. Studies of similar projects by risk specialists
B. Risk databases that may be available from industry sources
C. Review of vendor contracts to examine risks in past projects
D. Information on prior, similar projects

21 You are completing the qualitative risk analysis process with your project team and are relying on the risk management plan to help you determine the budget, schedule for risk management, and risk categories. You discover that the risk categories have not been created. When should the risk categories have been created?
A. Create work breakdown structure process
B. Plan risk management process
C. Risk identification process
D. Define scope process

22 The communication management plan contains all of the following EXCEPT:
A. Risk reporting formats
B. Escalation process of issues
C. Glossary of communication-related terms
D. Frequency of communication

23 During which of the following processes, probability and impact matrix is used?
A. Perform Qualitative Risk Analysis
B. Monitoring and Control Risks
C. Plan Risk Responses
D. Perform Quantitative Risk Analysis

24 Which of the following can best help a project manager during project execution?
A. Stakeholder analysis
B. Change Control Board
C. PMIS
D. Scope validation

25 What approach can a project manager use to improve the project's performance during qualitative risk analysis?
A. Focus on near-term risks first.
B. Create a risk breakdown structure and delegate the risk analysis to the appropriate project team members.
C. Focus on high-priority risks.
D. Analyse as many risks as possible regardless of who initiated the risk event.

26   What tools and techniques are used to estimate the overall risk exposure of the
      project?
      A. Advanced quantitative tools and specialised qualitative techniques
      B. Advanced quantitative tools and risk response techniques
      C. Decision trees and Monte Carlo simulations
      D. Risk ranking probability and impact matrices

27   Frank is the project manager of the NHQ project for his company. Frank is working
      with the project team, key stakeholders, and several subject matter experts on risks
      dealing with the new materials in the project. Frank wants to utilise a risk analysis
      method that will help the team to make decisions in the presence of the current
      uncertainty surrounding the new materials. Which risk analysis approach can Frank
      use to create an approach to make decisions in the presence of uncertainty?
      A. Monte Carlo Technique
      B. Qualitative risk analysis process
      C. Quantitative risk analysis process
      D. Delphi Technique

28   If a project manager wants to report on the actual project results versus the planned
      results which should be used: -
      A. Trend reports
      B. Forecasting reports
      C. Status reports
      D. Variance reports

29   You are the project manager of the KJH Project and are working with your project
      team to plan the risk responses. Consider that your project has a budget of $500,000
      and is expected to last six months. Within the KJH Project you have identified a risk
      event that has a probability of .70 and has a cost impact of $350,000. When it comes
      to creating a risk response for this event what is the risk exposure of the event that
      must be considered for the cost of the risk response?
      A. The risk exposure of the event is $245,000.
      B. The risk exposure of the event is $500,000.
      C. The risk exposure of the event is $350,000.
      D. The risk exposure of the event is $850,000.

30   Fred is the project manager of the CPS project. He is working with his project team to
      prioritise the identified risks within the CPS project. He and the team are prioritising
      risks for further analysis or action by assessing and combining the risks probability of
      occurrence and impact. What process is Fred completing?
      A. Risk identification
      B. Perform qualitative analysis
      C. Perform quantitative analysis
      D. Risk Breakdown Structure creation

31 The cost performance index (CPI) of a project is 0.6 and the schedule performance index (SPI) is 0.71. The project has 625 work packages and is being completed over a four-year period. The team members are very inexperienced, and the project received little support for proper planning. Which of the following is the BEST thing to do?
A. Update risk identification and analysis.
B. Spend more time improving the cost estimates.
C. Remove as many work packages as possible.
D. Reorganise the responsibility assignment matrix.

32 Virginia is the project manager for her organisation. She has hired a subject matter expert to interview the project stakeholders on certain identified risks within the project. The subject matter expert will assess the risk event with what specific goal in mind?
A. To determine the level of probability and impact for each risk event
B. To determine the bias of the risk event based on each person interviewed
C. To determine the probability and cost of the risk event
D. To determine the validity of each risk event

33 A mathematical analysis that shows the risks that have the most potential impact on the project is termed:
A. Expected Monetary Value
B. Monte Carlo Simulation
C. Utility Function
D. Sensitivity Analysis

34 You are the project manager of the NHJ project for your company. This project has a budget at completion of $1,650,000 and you are 60 percent complete. According to the project plan, however, the project should be 65 percent complete. In this project you have spent $995,000 to reach this point of completion. There is a risk that this project may be late so you have taken some measures to recover the project schedule. Management would like to know, based on current performance, what the estimate at completion for this project will be. What is the estimate at completion?
A. $1,650,000
B. $1,666,667
C. $663,333
D. -$8,333

35   You work as a project manager for BlueWell Inc. You are concerned with the risks on the project with the lack of allocation and detail on resource assignment. You want to create a visual diagram, which can depict the resources that will be used within the project. Which of the following diagrams will you create to accomplish the task?
A. Roles and responsibility matrix
B. Work breakdown structure
C. Resource breakdown structure
D. RACI chart

36   The term used to define a risk that is due to a catastrophe or a force of nature is considered:
A. Force-majeure
B. Lasses-faire
C. Utility function
D. None of the above

37   During qualitative risk analysis you want to define the risk urgency assessment. All of the following are indicators of risk priority except for which one?
A. Cost of the project
B. Risk rating
C. Warning signs
D. Symptoms

38   Amy is the project manager for her company. In her current project the organisation has a very low tolerance for risk events that will affect the project schedule. Management has asked Amy to consider the affect of all the risks on the project schedule. What approach can Amy take to create a bias against risks that will affect the schedule of the project?
A. She can create an overall project rating scheme to reflect the bias towards risks that affect the project schedule.
B. She can filter all risks based on their affect on schedule versus other project objectives.
C. She can have the project team pad their time estimates to alleviate delays in the project schedule.
D. She can shift risk-laden activities that affect the project schedule from the critical path as much as possible.

39   You are finding it difficult to evaluate the exact cost impact of risks. You should evaluate on a(n):
A. Quantitative basis.
B. Numerical basis.
C. Qualitative basis.
D. Econometric basis.

40   While planning an end-user feedback event, the project manager became concerned
      that too many of the end-users invited to the event would show. More RSVPs were
      received than actual seats available. This was strategically planned, since a statistical
      percentage of individuals that RSVP do not show, but the project manager recognised
      that a risk did exist. While more end-user participants would be a benefit to the project,
      the project management team would need to be prepared to deal with the extra
      number of participants. What type of risk is this?
      A. Business Risk
      B. Pure Risk
      C. Partial Risk
      D. Organisational Risk

nswers

C   The formulae that must be remembered is: -

Expected = (Optimistic + (4 * Most Likely) + Pessimistic) / 6

So plugging the numbers, you should get 60. The only confusion was maybe the order of the numbers!

2   D   As the project is performing quantitative analysis by using the decision tree, the next logical tool and technique to use is Monte Carlo analysis as now a simulation on the results can be performed

3   A   the answer here is Option A as this is a leadership / motivation theory

4   C   Sensitivity analysis is quantitative analysis technique helps in finding which risks can have most impact on the project and Tornado diagram is the most common way of representing sensitivity analysis. It is not used for Monitor and Control risks process.
Option A – Risk audits is the tool to examine and document the effectiveness of risk responses in dealing with identified risks and their root causes, as well as the effectiveness of risk management system.
Option B – Variance and Trend Analysis is technique for monitor and control risk which can be used to find variance analysis to compare planned and actual results.
Option D -Reserve Analysis is used to compare the remaining contingency reserve and amount of risk remaining at any time in the project in order to determine if the remaining reserve is adequate.

5   B   When you read the options, it is Option B that is the only one that makes sense to having a constructive qualitative analysis as part of the project

6   D   The process on how, where and what to use as part of the project risk management is contained in the risk management plan

7   C   Options B and C are the only possible answers. Mitigation strategies are planned for identified risks. In this case the risk has already happened. Therefore, the meeting is to determine a workaround.

8   D   Variance and trend analysis involves using performance data to review the trends in the project's execution for monitoring overall project performance. The tools and techniques used for performing variance and trend analysis include: earned value analysis, variance analysis and trend analysis.

9   A   The Expected Monetary Value (EMV) is 10% x 100,000 = 10,000, which is the same as the insurance cost. Therefore, A is the correct option.

10 D This is a general questions and all answers are correct but one must be chosen. The reason why ALL project members are involved is because of project priorities. The other three options are specific to a part of the audience.

11 D A) Choice A is incorrect. A weighting system is used for comparing different sellers against the defined evaluation criteria
B) Choice B is incorrect because A screening system is used to eliminate sellers that do not meet the minimum criteria
C) An expected value is a method of evaluating probabilities on decision trees and this cannot be applied in this scenario and thus choice C is wrong
D) Independent estimates are prepared to compare cost estimates among several potential sellers, which can help to uncover any significant difference in understanding of scope between the buyer and the supplier. Often-time a bid that is way over or way under the mean compared to other seller's responses will signify that there is a misunderstanding in scope.

12 A Procurement is a key theme on the exam and it is good to understand the contract types and associated risk: -
1. Fixed prices contracts is where the vendor / seller is accepting the risk
2. Cost price or Cost plus contracts is where the risk is shared but the project can be accepting of the majority of risks
3. Time and Materials (T&M) contracts is where the project is fully accepting the risk.
Given this, the answer is either Option A or Option C. However, the cost plus percentage fee places more risk on the project than the cost plus incentive fee

13 D The formulae that must be remembered is: -

Standard Deviation = (Pessimistic - Optimistic) / 6

So plugging the numbers, you should get 4.

14 C Risk identification is performed after performing the risk management plan.

15 A John is using the Delphi technique to identify risks

16 A This is essentially an Earned Value Question which are a rarity on the exam but it is still good to know how to execute this. The first part of this questions indicates that the contingency response is used in the index is less than 90% (0.9). The current status is that we are 65% complete with $175,000 spent. This means the EV is (0.65 x $275,000) $178,500 and the Cost Performance Index (178,500 / 175,000) which is 1.02

17 C The best answer here is Monte Carlo analysis as this is based off a range analysis / PERT which allows understanding of the variances between optimistic and pessimistic

8	C	This is an example of consultative leadership where the project manager is fostering a culture of involvement and consultation
9	A	Let's assume the duration to be X days. 12 * X = 1000 + 4 * X , 8X = 1000 , X = 125.This means that if the ladder is used for any duration equal or greater than 125 days it is economical to purchase rather than lease - so in other words to lease the duration should be equal to or less than 125 days - so option A is the right answer
20	C	The vendor contracts is a current artefact that the project has created. All other options are lessons learnt or corporate knowledge which are part of the Organisational Process Assets
21	B	The answer is certainly not Option A or Option D. The categories should have been defined prior to the risk identification. So this leaves Option B as the correct answer
22	A	This is need to know the basics of what a communication plan contains:
23	A	The probability and impact matrix is used during qualitative analysis. This is a standard risk process question focusing on use of tool and techniques
24	C	Choice A is incorrect, as stakeholder analysis should have been completed during the project planning processes. Choice B is also incorrect. CCBs can assist the project manager, but not as much as the control and assistance offered through a PMIS. Choice C is correct. A PMIS can assist the project manager the most during project execution. It does not replace the role of the project manager. This is a tool and technique of direct and manage project execution. The other tool and technique is expert judgment. Choice D is incorrect. Scope validation is proof of the project work, not an assistant to the project manager.
25	C	Qualitative analysis is focused on generating a prioritised set of risks that allows concerted analysis and response. The approach to qualitative analysis may be to do an iterative process of prioritisation
26	A	Evaluate the attributes of identified risks using advanced quantitative tools and specialised qualitative techniques in order to estimate overall risk exposure of the project.
27	C	Frank is using a decision tree analysis approach to the risk which is part of quantitative analysis #
28	D	The correct answer is D as this shows the gap between plan and actual
29	A	This is a simple question and the answer is 0.7 x $350,000 which is Option A
30	B	Ask yourself the question, where in the risk management process does a project manager 'prioritise the identified risks '. This is done during the qualitative analysis

31 A This is not about the question but rather the options. There is only one option that be of help to the team in the current situation they face and that is option A.

32 A The key part of this question is the situation of where the risk are identified and Virginia is now interviewing the project stakeholders. With this in mind the next step of the process is to perform qualitative analysis which is the impact and probability assessment

33 D The correct answer is "Sensitivity Analysis"

34 B An Earned Value question, a very simple way to determine the answer this question is: -
- You are actually 60% complete
- You should be 65% complete
- From this you can determine that the schedule is not progressing well
- The CPI = EV (990,000) / AC (995,000). Eva is calculated as 0.60 x 1,650,000
- The EAC = Budget (1,650,000) / CPI (0.99)
- EAC = 1,666,666.67

35 C This is not a question on risk management processes but more to do with the tools and techniques for project management. The questions asks for a visual diagram to understand resources which is the core objective of the RBS (Resource Breakdown Structure).

36 A A force-majeure is a term referring to a risk that is due to a catastrophe or a force of nature

37 A The cost of the project is not a risk indicator. This is an Earned Value or Budget indicator

38 A When biases are discussed, they are linked to understanding and reflect probability and impact. To reflect any bias into the project, Amy should focus on the risk probability and impact assessments being doing for the project

39 C If you cannot determine an exact cost impact to the event, use qualitative estimates such as Low, Medium, High, etc.

40 B This is an example of pure risk. The risk can have a positive influence as well as a negative influence.

RMP® Simulated Sample Exams

RMP® Sample Exam 1

Answer Sheet

Question	Answer	Correction	Question	Answer	Correction	Question	Answer	Correction
1			21			41		
2			22			42		
3			23			43		
4			24			44		
5			25			45		
6			26			46		
7			27			47		
8			28			48		
9			29			49		
10			30			50		
11			31					
12			32					
13			33					
14			34					
15			35					
16			36					
17			37					
18			38					
19			39					
20			40					

Exam

1   You are working with Anna on your project to determine and map the probability
     distributions of risk within the project. You have indicated that you will use the uniform
     distribution method for a portion of the project. Which part of your project is most likely
     to have a uniform risk distribution?
     A. Late completion stages of a project
     B. Project phases that deal with "cutover" technologies
     C. Early concept stage of design
     D. Project initiating

2   Which of the following is not an output of the qualitative risk analysis?
     A. A prioritised list of risks for a given project objective based on the probability and
     impact matrix of the objective
     B. A watch list of low-priority risks
     C. A list of risks prioritised based on the total effect of each risk on the overall project
     objectives
     D. A list of trends in the analysis results

3   The probability of risk occurring is highest during which stage of project management?
     A. Initiating
     B. Planning
     C. Executing
     D. Closing

4   After much excitement and hard work, the procurement statement of work for the
     project is completed. Even after gaining agreement that the procurement statement of
     work is complete, the project manager is still concerned whether it actually addresses
     all the buyer's needs. The project manager is about to attend the bidder conference.
     He asks you for advice on what to do during the session. Which of the following is the
     BEST advice you can give him?
     A. You do not need to attend this session. The contract manager will hold it.
     B. Make sure you negotiate project scope.
     C. Make sure you give all the sellers enough time to ask questions. They may not
     want to ask questions while their competitors are in the room.
     D. Let the project sponsor handle the meeting so you can be the good guy in the
     negotiation session.

5   The process of developing strategies to reduce the threat of uncertainties to project
     objectives is a process called:
     A. Risk Communication
     B. Risk Analysis
     C. Risk Identification
     D. Risk Response Planning

During which of the following processes is a probability and impact matrix used?
A. Perform Qualitative Risk Analysis
B. Monitoring and Control Risks
C. Risk Management Planning
D. Perform Quantitative Risk Analysis

Your organisation, as part of its enterprise environmental factors, has established risk governance to be implemented in each project. Part of this governance is the reassessment of risks within each project. How much detail and repetition in approach for risks to be reassessed for probability and impact?
A. Each risk reassessment should go into the same depth as the original risk assessment activity.
B. The probability and impact of risk event should determine the level of reassessment throughout the project lifecycle.
C. The amount of detail of repetition that is appropriate depends on how the project progresses relative to its objectives.
D. The level of detail and reassessment should reflect the priority of the project.

Todd is the project manager of the EST project for his company. His organisation has established certain rules in the enterprise environmental factors which affect the approach that Todd takes in managing his project. One of the rules requires Todd to consider the risk attitude of the stakeholders participating in risk analysis. Why must risk attitude be considered as a part of risk analysis?
A. Risk attitude can affect the measurement of probability and impact.
B. Risk attitude can establish a stakeholder's influence over project decisions.
C. Risk attitude identifies stakeholders that are hygiene seekers or motivation seekers.
D. Risk attitude establishes stakeholders as positive or negative stakeholders.

You are the project manager of RTF project for your organisation. You are working with your project team and several key stakeholders to create a diagram that shows causal factors for an effect to be solved. What diagramming technique are you using as a part of the risk identification process?
A. Cause and effect diagrams
B. System or process flow charts
C. Predecessor and successor diagramming
D. Influence diagrams

10   The project stakeholders have reviewed your project and feel that the cost accuracy, risk exposure and duration estimates need to be improved and that the projects expected end date is too far into the future. What should you do first?

A. Re-interview the subject matter experts (SME's) and ask for better estimates.

B. Re-examine the WBS to see if it can be further decomposed, to allow for better estimating on cost and duration.

C. Tell your stakeholders that your estimates are sufficient. They are just stakeholders and have no real understanding of your project.

D. Reduce all the cost and time estimates by 20% based on your feedback.

11   When involved in project negotiations, non-verbal communication skills are of: -

A. Only important if required

B. Little importance

C. Major importance

D. Important to the point of engaging stakeholders

12   You are working with your project stakeholders to identify risks within the JKP Project. You want to use an approach to engage the stakeholders to increase the breadth of the identified risks by including internally generated risk. Which risk identification approach is most suited for this goal?

A. Delphi Technique

B. SWOT analysis

C. Assumptions analysis

D. Brainstorming

13   Which of the following is NOT an input for the Qualitative Risk Analysis process?

A. Risk management plan

B. Enterprise environmental factors

C. Risk register

D. Stakeholder register

14   Risk categories can BEST be described as:

A. A group of project risks.

B. A group of negative risks.

C. A group of potential root causes of risk.

D. A group of potential causes of risk.

15   Which of the following documents is described in the statement below? "It is developed along with all processes of the risk management. It contains the results of the qualitative risk analysis, quantitative risk analysis, and risk response planning."

A. Risk management plan

B. Project charter

C. Risk register

D. Quality management plan

6   During the creation of the risk management plan, you decide to start by analysing the
     risk tolerance levels of the organisation and of stakeholders. What information are you
     most likely to utilise?
     A. Project management plan
     B. Risk management plan
     C. Organisational process assets
     D. Enterprise environmental factors

7   The impact of risk occurring is lowest during which stage of project management?
     A. Initiating
     B. Planning
     C. Executing
     D. Closing

8   You have just finished updating the risk register with the prioritised list of risks. What
     risk management process are you currently in?
     A. Identify Risks
     B. Perform Qualitative Risk Analysis
     C. Perform Quantitative Risk Analysis
     D. Plan Risk Responses

9   A diagramming technique that shows causal influences, time ordering of events, and
     an expectation of outcomes considering a set of variables is considered:
     A. An Influence Diagram
     B. An Ishikawa Diagram
     C. A Flow Chart
     D. A Scatter Diagram

10   Jenny is the project manager for the NBT projects. She is working with the project
     team and several subject matter experts to perform the quantitative risk analysis
     process. During this process she and the project team uncover several risks events
     that were not previously identified. What should Jenny do with these risk events?
     A. The events should be entered into qualitative risk analysis.
     B. The events should be determined if they need to be accepted or responded to.
     C. The events should be entered into the risk register.
     D. The events should continue on with quantitative risk analysis.

21   Which of the following statements BEST describes Checklist Analysis?
A. Involves identifying an issue, determining what the cause is for the issue, and resolving it.
B. Involve the participation of subject matter experts, stakeholders and other participants to identify risks.
C. Evaluates whether the assumptions used to identify risks are valid, accurate, and consistent.
D. Makes sure that all items within the project have been considered for risk.

22   A risk is characterised by:
A. Category of Risk and Risk Response
B. Risk Event, Risk Qualitative Analysis and Risk Strategy
C. Type of Risk, Impact and Response
D. Risk Event, Probability, and Impact

23   Your project spans the entire organisation. You would like to assess the risk of the project but are worried that some of the managers involved in the project could affect the outcome of any risk identification meeting. Your worry is based on the fact that some employees would not want to publicly identify risk events that could make their supervisors look bad. You would like a method that would allow participants to anonymously identify risk events. What risk identification method could you use?
A. Delphi technique
B. Isolated pilot groups
C. SWOT analysis
D. Root cause analysis

24   During execution in a project to build a major road bridge, your team found a major flaw in the technical drawings. On an ad-hoc base, they had to find and implement a workaround to avoid delays and mitigate technical problems. What should you do next?
A. Meticulously document the problem and the workaround to create a requested change to the project management plan
B. The workaround was performed on a technical level only. As long as it does not influence the function of the bridge or the configuration of the project, a change request is not necessary.
C. A formal change request side is not needed. Create some additional documents describing the workaround and ask the team to sign them.
D. It is normal in projects that during project execution inconsistencies arise between planning documents and actual implementation. This is no problem as long as the functional status of the product is maintained.

5   A project manager has just finished the risk response plan for a U.S. $387,000 engineering project. Which of the following should he probably do NEXT?
A. Determine the overall risk rating of the project.
B. Begin to analyse the risks that show up in the project drawings.
C. Add work packages to the project work breakdown structure.
D. Hold a project risk reassessment.

6   You are a project manager for one of many projects in a large and important program. At a high-level status meeting, you note that another project manager has reported her project on schedule. Looking back on your project over the last few weeks, you remember many deliverables from the other project that arrived late. What should you do?
A. Meet with the program manager.
B. Develop a risk control plan.
C. Discuss the issue with your boss.
D. Meet with the other project manager.

7   Sammy is the project manager for her organisation. She would like to rate each risk based on its probability and effect on time, cost, and scope. Harry, a project team member, has never done this before and thinks Sammy is wrong to attempt this approach. Harry says that an accumulative risk score should be created, not three separate risk scores. Who is correct in this scenario?
A. Harry is correct, because the risk probability and impact considers all objectives of the project.
B. Harry is correct, the risk probability and impact matrix is the only approach to risk assessment.
C. Sammy is correct, because organisations can create risk scores for each objective of the project.
D. Sammy is correct, because she is the project manager.

8   Jonathon is a new project manager and is introduced into the project at an early stage. Jonathon wants to liaise with stakeholders of other projects by using communication techniques and sharing information on project risk performance. Which technique should Jonathon use?
A. Brainstorming techniques
B. Basic risk identification tools
C. SWOT analysis
D. Cause and Effect analysis

9   A risk register is an output of this process:
A. Quantitative Risk Analysis
B. Risk Identification
C. Risk Management Analysis
D. Qualitative Risk Analysis

30   Jane is the project manager of the GBB project for her company. In the current project a vendor has offered the project a ten percent discount based if they will order 100 units for the project. It is possible that the GBB Project may need the 100 units, but the cost of the units is not a top priority for the project. Jane documents the offer and tells the vendor that they will keep the offer in mind and continue with the project as planned. What risk response has been given in this project?
      A. Acceptance
      B. Enhance
      C. Exploiting
      D. Sharing

31   Which Risk Response strategy can involve using tools such as insurance, performance bonds, warranties or guarantees?
      A. Avoid
      B. Transfer
      C. Mitigate
      D. Accept

32   All of the following are tools and techniques of the Identify Risks process EXCEPT:
      A. Risk urgency assessment
      B. Documentation reviews
      C. Assumptions analysis
      D. Cause and effect diagrams

33   A project has a tight budget when you begin negotiating with a seller for a piece of equipment. The seller has told you that the equipment price is fixed. Your manager has told you to negotiate the cost with the seller. What is your BEST course of action?
      A. Make a good faith effort to find a way to decrease the cost.
      B. Postpone negotiations until you can convince your manager to change his mind.
      C. Hold the negotiations, but only negotiate other aspects of the project.
      D. Cancel the negotiations.

34   You are the project manager of the NHQ Project for your company. You have completed qualitative and quantitative analysis of your identified project risks and you would now like to find an approach to increase project opportunities and to reduce threats within the project. What project management process would best help you?
      A. Monitor and control project risks
      B. Create a risk governance approach
      C. Create the project risk register
      D. Plan risk responses

85 You are managing a project and based on risk identification - you feel very confident that the project should run smoothly. The next day the lead architect indicates a risk which was not envisioned. He indicates a 10% possibility of the risk occurring and the effort involved of choosing an alternate path worth $2000. The side effect of alternate path implementation is that a lot of testing efforts would get reduced worth $4500 and the possibility being 30%.What would be the EMV?
A. -$200
B. $1350
C. $1150
D. $1550

86 Which of the following is an output of the Identify Risks process.
A. Lessons Learned
B. Checklists
C. Risk Register
D. SWOT Analysis

87 How should risk ownership be communicated to project stakeholders?
A. Risk Breakdown Structure
B. Work Breakdown Structure
C. Responsibility Assignments
D. Risk Management Plan

88 The project is coming to a close and an analysis of lesson learnt is finally been completed. A project stakeholder mentions that the project communication was not what she expected it to be and it came as a surprise that the project communicated so frequently during the project. As the project manager, a root cause analysis should be done on which of the following?
A. The technology and requirements of the stakeholder group
B. The Organisational Process Assets to understand the communication guidelines
C. The level of resistance to project communication
D. The process of communication planning

89 You work as the project manager for BlueWell Inc. You are monitoring the project performance. You want to make a decision to change the project plan to eliminate a risk in order to protect the project objectives. Which of the following strategies will you use to tackle the risk?
A. Risk mitigation
B. Risk avoidance
C. Risk acceptance
D. Risk transference

40   A project manager working for a mid-level software company is in the process of executing the project work. During risk management planning, the team had discovered 42 risks that require some form of action or response. Over the coming weeks, the time to implement these actions would take place. During which stage of this project would the impact of risk be at its highest?
A. Initiating
B. Planning
C. Executing
D. Closing

41   What risk identification technique allows participants to identify the project risks and to remain anonymous?
A. Influence diagrams
B. Assumptions analysis
C. Surveys
D. Delphi technique

42   Techniques such as risk-based earned value and risk-based critical chain analysis are associated with which risk management area:
A. Risk Monitor and Control
B. Risk Response Planning
C. Quantitative Risk Analysis
D. Qualitative Risk Analysis

43   Your company has an emergency and needs contracted work done as soon as possible. Under these circumstances, which of the following would be the MOST helpful to add to the contract?
A. A clear procurement statement of work
B. Requirements as to which subcontractors can be used
C. Incentives
D. A force majeure clause

44   You are the project manager of the NKJ Project for your company. The project's success or failure will have a significant impact on your organisation's profitability for the coming year. Management has asked you to identify the risk events and communicate the event's probability and impact as early as possible in the project. Management wants to avoid risk events and needs to analyse the cost-benefits of each risk event in this project. What term is assigned to the low-level of stakeholder tolerance in this project?
A. Mitigation-ready project management
B. Risk utility function
C. Risk avoidance
D. Risk-reward mentality

5   Your procurement department has obtained independent estimates. The vendor's proposal is substantially different than the independent estimates. All of the following are true except:
A. The Contract SOW was not detailed enough.
B. The vendor failed to respond according to the terms of the proposal.
C. The vendor failed to respond to all items in the Contract SOW.
D. The vendor failed to respond to all items in the contract.

6   You and your project team are identifying the risks that may exist within your project. Some of the risks are small risks that won't affect your project much if they happen. What should you do with these identified risk events?
A. All risks must have a valid, documented risk response.
B. These risks can be accepted.
C. These risks can be added to a low priority risk watch list.
D. These risks can be dismissed.

7   You are the project manager of the NNQ Project for your company and are working with your project team to define contingency plans for the risks within your project. Mary, one of your project team members, asks what a contingency plan is. Which of the following statements best defines what a contingency response is?
A. Some responses are designed for use only if certain events occur.
B. Some responses have a cost and a time factor to consider for each risk event.
C. Some responses must counteract pending risk events.
D. Quantified risks should always have contingency responses.

8   You have just completed make-or-buy analysis, and you and your team make a "buy decision" for a sub-project of the project. Upon knowing this decision, your manager recommends that you give the sub-project to one of the companies that you have worked with many times because your organisation has always enjoyed a good relationship with this company; this company is very reputable. What should you do under the circumstances?
A. Follow the manager's recommendations.
B. Determine whether this company truly has the capacity to execute and finish this sub-project.
C. Reject the manager's recommendations and keep this company out of the list of potential sellers.
D. Examine the relationship between this company and the manager.

9   Which of the following contract types places the greatest risk on the seller
A. Cost plus fixed fee contract
B. Cost plus incentive fee contract
C. Firm fixed price contract
D. Fixed price incentive contract

50   You are the project manager of the GHG project for your company. You have identified the project risks, completed qualitative and quantitative analysis, and created risk responses. You also need to document how and when risk audits will be performed in the project. Where will you define the frequency of risk audits?

A. Risk response plan

B. Quality management plan

C. Risk management plan

D. Schedule management plan

nswers

C This is a simple tool and technique question. In others words, where will you using statistical analysis. This is what quantitative analysis performs

C Option C is the correct answer because you need to perform quantitative risk analysis to create a list of risks prioritised based on the total effect of each risk on the overall project objectives. Options A, B, and D are incorrect because these are the possible output items from the qualitative risk analysis

C Re-read the question if you got this wrong. The question asks 'The probability of risk occurring is highest during which stage of project management'. The answer to this is the Execution Stage of the project

C This question is really asking about the objective of a bidder conference. Even though there is a narrative on the statement of work, it does not contribute to the question. The objective of a bidder conference is option C

D This is a simple question and relies on a basic understanding of the risk management process

A The answer here is Option A, the probability and impact matric is prepared during the risk management planning process and used during the risk qualitative analysis process

C This is a question where the appropriate answer is the one that reflects that risk management is not a standard process but is based on the correct detail based on priority and need. Option C covers this while the other Options are too rigid

A The answer to this question is either Option A or Option B. the simple fact is that the risk attitude assessment is based on understand probability and impact which is Option A. Option B is focused more to the assessment of the impact of the stakeholder on the project itself

A This is a great question as you are right to think that Option A and D are two diagramming techniques for risk identification. The question does ask the technique for to create a diagram that shows causal factors for an effect to be solved which is cause and effect. Hence Option A is the correct answer

0 B Answer B is correct. If your cost accuracy and duration estimates need to be improved, then that could tell you that you're current estimates are not accurate. Thus the first thing you should do is re-examine the WBS to see if it can be further decomposed, to allow for better estimating on cost and duration. You might also do A, but you would first re-examine the WBS.

1 C Non-verbal includes body language (kinetics) and pitch and tone (para-linguistic) and account for 90 - 92% of communication

12	B	The questions asks that you want to use an approach to engage the stakeholders to increase the breadth of the identified risks by including internally generated risk. While all the options are risk identification tools, the only option that looks at the different categories of risk (opportunities and threats) is the SWOT analysis
13	D	The stakeholder register is the option that is the least helpful as an input for Qualitative Analysis. All the other three options would be required for various reasons
14	A	Risk categories are associated with categorising project risks
15	C	One of the outputs of risk identification, qualitative risk analysis and quantitative risk analysis is the risk register. In some cases the risk register is updated but it is still an output
16	C	Revisit the question "During the creation of the risk management plan, you decide to start by analysing the risk tolerance levels of the organisation and of stakeholders". Where do you think you would find how to do this and previous experience of this activity, the answer is Organisational Process Assets
17	D	This is a great question to test your knowledge of the risk lifecycle. The impact of the risk is the lowest at closing because at this point the project is being delivery, the budget spent and the resource are being released
18	B	The risk are prioritised which means that qualitative analysis is being performed
19	A	Page 287 of the PMBOK Guide 4th Edition. Section 11.2.2.5 Identify Risks: Tools and Techniques: Diagramming Techniques
20	C	Jenny has just completed the risk identification and the questions is asking what should be done with the risk events. The answer is to log them and then the next process step is analysis
21	D	When you look at this question, it is asking what Checklist Analysis is. Option A, B and C are all dedicated risk or issues management activities. Option D is the reason why checklists are used
22	D	The correct answer is "Risk Event, Probability, and Impact"
23	A	This is a straightforward question and should not be posing a problem if you are coming near to your exam. The answer is option A and this is what Delphi technique is or it is sometimes called Wideband Delphi Technique
24	A	Without doubt A should be the answer as it is the only option that follows process

5   C   In order to identify the answer to this question, you think inputs and outputs and position risk response planning within that model.
Risk response planning is the final step of the risk management planning cycle and the act of risk identification, qualitative risk analysis (choice A and B) have been completed. The natural thing to do once the risk response plan is in place is to update the project plan with the outputs, this is reflected by updating the WBS (choice C). PMI does not refer to risk-re-assessment. To re-assess a risk, the project manager goes through the risk management cycle again.

6   D   This is something that should be addressed directly with the other project manager as you do not evidence of this delay and should raise your concerns with the responsible project manager

7   C   This is a question that needs to be read a number of times. It is one of the more difficult questions on the exam, so if you can answer this, you can answer anything. The first thing is that Sammy is correct as each risk can be assessed individually which is Option C. The final point here is that Option D is not correct as it supplies no rationale

8   A   The correct answer here is Brainstorming as all of the other options are associated with the facilitation of the risk process and not with engagement / communication skills

9   B   The risk register will appear for the first time once risk identification is completed. However, updates to the risk register will happen during qualitative and quantitative analysis

0   A   As this is not a top priority for the project and for Jane, the risk is being accepted

1   B   Risk transference is a risk response strategy whereby the project team shifts the impact of a threat to a third party, together with ownership of the response

2   A   The answer is 'Urgency Assessments' as this is a Qualitative Analysis tool

3   A   There is always a way to decrease costs on a project. How about offering to feature the seller in your next television ad? The best answer is A

4   D   You have completed qualitative and quantitative analysis of your identified project risks and you would now like to find an approach to increase project opportunities and to reduce threats within the project. The step to realise this is the risk response planning stage which is Option D

5   C   The correct answer is $1150.In the case of the rework effort the EMV is -$200.The EMV of the side effect is $1350.So the total EMV is $1150.

6   C   Risk Register is the only output of the Risk identification process.

37   C   Risk ownership is promoted by proactively communicating roles and responsibilities and engaging project team members in the development of risk responses in order to improve risk response execution. You may argue that Option D is the better answer, but Option C is specific to communicating ownership

38   B   The answer here is Option B. This is a very close call between B and D, while Option D is not correct the better answer here is B. The communication guidelines, principles and policies should be part of the Organisational Process Assets and these are used to form the way the project will work. It must be assumed that the stakeholder disagreeing with the communicational protocol in the project was involved in the communication planning process. The focus of the investigation (root cause) should be done at an organisational level rather than a project level

39   B   You want to make a decision to change the project plan to eliminate a risk in order to protect the project objectives. The question asks which risk response strategy are you using here. The strategy is elimination which is the same as risk avoidance

40   A   The risk is always the highest at the start of the project which is initiation

41   D   The answer here is Option D and this is the definition of the Delphi technique or sometimes called Wideband Delphi

42   C   Advanced quantitative risk analysis tools and techniques includes but are not limited to, integrated cost/schedule analysis, advanced Monte Carlo analysis, system dynamics, bowtie analysis, analytical hierarchy process, risk-based earned value analysis, risk-based critical chain analysis, and multi-factor regression analysis, modelling techniques, advanced risk metric analysis [including statistical process control

43   C   The inclusion of incentive means that the seller will be bound by a performance related payment scheme which will aid any emergency work

44   C   Risk tolerance is also known as utility. This is a standard term and definition

45   A   In this question, you must assume that the vendor responded with honesty and integrity to all items in the Tender Documentation. Secondly, the contract has not being issued yet (choice D) and hence this option is invalid whereas the 'terms of proposal' is not a PMI procurement document (Choice B). the choice is between A and C and given the honest relationship that exists in the procurement lifecycle, the onus should be on the documentation (Choice A)

46   C   As the risks are small risks that won't affect your project much if they happen, they should be added to the low-priority watchlist

47   A   Contingency is essentially there to take care of any risk that may occur. Given this explanation, the more obvious answer for contingency is Option A

8   B   Even though your manager has given a direction, you must still continue with the procurement process which would mean the evaluation of the company's capability.

9   C   The first to do is identify that the buyer is the project and the seller is the vendor / contractor. Anything that is fixed price is a risk for the seller and answer C should be chosen as it is the tightest type of contract from a buyer's perspective

0   C   All information with regarding the process, frequency and structure of project risk management is contained in the risk management plan

RMP® Sample Exam 2

Answer Sheet

Question	Answer	Correction	Question	Answer	Correction	Question	Answer	Correction
1			21			41		
2			22			42		
3			23			43		
4			24			44		
5			25			45		
6			26			46		
7			27			47		
8			28			48		
9			29			49		
10			30			50		
11			31					
12			32					
13			33					
14			34					
15			35					
16			36					
17			37					
18			38					
19			39					
20			40					

Exam

1   You work as the project manager for Bluewell Inc. Your project has several risks that will affect several stakeholder requirements. Which project management plan will define who will be available to share information on the project risks?
A. Risk Management Plan
B. Stakeholder management strategy
C. Resource Management Plan
D. Communications Management Plan

2   A system development project is nearing project closing when a previously unidentified risk is discovered. This could potentially affect the project's overall ability to deliver. What should be done NEXT?
A. Alert the project sponsor of potential impacts to cost, scope, or schedule.
B. Qualify the risk.
C. Mitigate this risk by developing a risk response plan.
D. Develop a workaround.

3   Regarding Delphi Technique all of the following statements are true except
A. It is a way to reach a consensus of experts.
B. Experts are identified but participate anonymously while a facilitator uses a questionnaire to solicit ideas.
C. The experts are encouraged by the facilitator to make direct contact with each other during the assessment process to create a higher number of feedback loops.
D The responses are submitted and are then circulated to the experts for further comment.

4   The area where your project is taking place has experienced a high level of theft over the past month. The facility houses over $500,000 worth of equipment that is important to the project, and moving the equipment to a new location is not an option. Aside from a high-level alarm system, you also decide to purchase additional insurance to cover the equipment, should it get stolen. What type of risk is this?
A. Pure Risk
B. Business Risk
C. Organisational Risk
D. Project Risk

5   You are responsible for ensuring that your seller's performance meets contractual requirements. For effective contract administration, you should:
A. Hold a bidders conference
B. Establish the appropriate contract type
C. Implement the contract change control system
D. Develop a statement of work

During which of the following processes is a probability and impact matrix prepared?
A. Perform Qualitative Risk Analysis
B. Monitoring and Control Risks
C. Risk Management Planning
D. Perform Quantitative Risk Analysis

You are holding a weekly status meeting with stakeholders and are going through the to-do list and a list of actions items from the previous meeting. Some of the stakeholders are completely unaware of these action items and start raising concerns about how they suddenly appeared. Upon further questioning you realise that these stakeholders were absent during the last meeting due to scheduling conflicts. Which of these statements would best describe what should have been done to prevent this misunderstanding?
A. You should have updated the Work Breakdown Structure with the follow up tasks from the last meeting
B. You should have sent out an agenda prior to the meeting to clearly point out what the action items were from the previous meeting
C. You should have sent out meeting minutes after the last meeting to all stakeholders that were invited (whether or not they attended)
D. You should have briefed the stakeholders that did not attend the last meeting just prior to the start of this meeting

Which of the following is a primary source of risk identification gathering?
A. Interviewing
B. Delphi Technique
C. Brainstorming
D. Documentation Reviews

While conducting risk management planning, the project manager led the meeting participants, which included project team members and stakeholders, in a collaborative effort to break down the risk categories into subcategories. The end result was displayed as a hierarchical structure, containing the risk categories and subcategories. The project manager and meeting participants are utilising which of the following?
A. Work breakdown structure
B. Risk category structure
C. Risk breakdown structure
D. Resource breakdown structure

10   You are the project manager of the NHH project for your company. You have completed the first round of risk management planning and have created four outputs of the risk response planning process. Which one of the following is NOT an output of the risk response planning?
A. Risk register updates
B. Organisational process assets updates
C. Project document updates
D. Risk-related contract decisions

11   You produce risk management plan for the project on the basis of inputs such as project information, external factors, stakeholder inputs, and industry policies and procedures in order to define, fund, and staff effective risk management processes for the project that align with other project plans. What tool and technique have you used to develop this plan?
A. Delphi Technique
B. SWOT Analysis
C. Decision Trees
D. Risk attitude

12   What are workarounds in project risk management?
A. Workarounds are essentially the same as rework.
B. Workarounds are alternative strategies.
C. Workarounds are unplanned responses to emerging risks that were previously unidentified or accepted.
D. Workarounds are activities performed according to applicable contingency plans

13   During project execution, your project team delivers a project deliverable to the buyer. Your project team is happy as they have met the milestone but the buyer is not happy. The buyer refuses the deliverable as it does not meet the intended requirements as agreed when collecting requirements and then planning procurements. You review the documentation and find that the buyer is right. What is the BEST thing to do?
A. Explain that the contract is wrong and needs updating
B. Review the scope baseline with the responsible team
C. Issue a change order
D. Call a team meeting to identify what they understood

4   Jeff, a key stakeholder in your project, wants to know how the risk exposure for the risk events is calculated during quantitative risk analysis. He is worried about the risk exposure which is too low for the events surrounding his project requirements. How is the risk exposure calculated?

A. The risk exposure of a risk event is determined by historical information.

B. The probability of a risk event times the impact of a risk event determines the true risk exposure.

C. The probability of a risk event plus the impact of a risk event determines the true risk exposure.

D. The probability and impact of a risk event are gauged based on research and in-depth analysis.

5   Negotiations between two parties are becoming complex, so party A makes some notes that both parties sign. However, when the work is being done, party B claims that they are not required to provide an item they both agreed to during negotiations, because it was not included in the subsequent contract. In this case, party B is:

A. Incorrect, because both parties must comply with what they agreed upon.

B. Correct, because there was an offer.

C. Generally correct, because both parties are only required to perform what is in the contract.

D. Generally incorrect, because all agreements must be upheld.

6   Which of the following tools and techniques shows the impacts of one decision over another as well as the probability and cost of each risk along a logical path?

A. Simulation

B. Decision tree

C. Probability/impact risk matrix

D. Sensitivity analysis

7   Which of the following is not part of a performance report?

A. Current status of risks and issues

B. Explanation of % com rules and metrics

C. Work completed during the reporting period

D. Work to be completed during the next reporting period

8   You are the project manager of ABC project. Mid-way through the project a key component was stolen. This was not planned for. The team met after the event and managed to make the product work without the stolen component. This is an example of -

A. Risk mitigation

B. Transfer of risk

C. Work-around

D. Accepting the consequences passively

19 A project manager has just received news that symptoms were discovered signalling that a high rating risk is about to occur. This risk had the potential of bringing failure to the entire project. Due to the level of impact this risk would have on the project, all stakeholders needed to be informed. What should the project manager do?
   A. Hold a meeting with all of the stakeholders
   B. Call each stakeholder individually
   C. Meet with each stakeholder one-on-one
   D. Send an email to all stakeholders with the news

20 A project manager has assembled the project team, identified 56 risks on the project, determined what would trigger the risks, rated them on a risk rating matrix, tested their assumptions and assessed the quality of the data used. The team is continuing to move through the risk management process. What has the project manager forgotten to do?
   A. Simulation
   B. Risk mitigation
   C. Overall risk ranking for the project
   D. Involvement of other stakeholders

21 Which of the following is not an input to manage stakeholder engagement?
   A. Stakeholder management plan
   B. Project management plan
   C. Communications management plan
   D. Change log

22 You have just been assigned as project manager for a large manufacturing project. This one-year project is about halfway done. It involves five different sellers and 20 members of your company on the project team. You want to quickly review where the project now stands. Which of the following reports would be the MOST helpful in finding such information?
   A. Work status
   B. Progress
   C. Forecast
   D. Communications

23 Management reserves are used to handle which type of risk?
   A. Unknown unknowns
   B. Known unknowns
   C. Business risks
   D. Pure risks

4   Which of the following processes looks at the complex web of actors, rules, conventions, processes, and mechanisms concerned with how relevant risk information is collected, analysed and communicated, and how management decisions are taken?
A. Risk Communication
B. IRGC
C. Risk Response Planning
D. Risk Governance

5   You have been assigned to manage a project that deals with setting up a railway line connecting two cities. The project is complex with a lot of contracting involved. You and experts in your organisation are evaluating if the rail line alignment machinery should be purchased outright or if it would be better to lease. The cost of leasing the equipment is 1200 $ per day while the cost of an outright purchase is 96000 $ and a daily cost of 200 $.The duration of laying out the railway lines is scheduled to be an activity duration of 150 days. Should you purchase the machinery or be leased - which option would be more economical?
A. Lease the machinery as it will be cheaper by 84000 USD
B. Purchase the machinery as it its usage beyond the 80th day would be more cost effective to purchase rather than lease
C. Purchase the machinery as it its usage beyond the 96th day would be more cost effective to purchase rather than lease
D. Lease the machinery as it will be cheaper by 36000 USD

6   Which one of the following is the only output for the qualitative risk analysis process?
A. Enterprise environmental factors
B. Project management plan
C. Risk register updates
D. Organisational process assets

7   Joan is the project manager of the BTT project for her company. She has worked with her project to create risk responses for both positive and negative risk events within the project. As a result of this process Joan needs to update the project document updates. She has updated the assumptions log as a result of the findings and risk responses, but what other documentation will need to be updated as an output of risk response planning?
A. Scope statement
B. Lessons learned
C. Risk Breakdown Structure
D. Technical documentation

28 All of the following are processes within the Project Risk Management Knowledge Area EXCEPT:
A. Plan Risk Management
B. Identify Risks
C. Risk Analysis
D. Plan Risk Responses

29 Tom is the project manager for his organisation. In his project he has recently finished the risk response planning. He tells his manager that he will now need to update the cost and schedule baselines. Why would the risk response planning cause Tom the need to update the cost and schedule baselines?
A. New or omitted work as part of a risk response can cause changes to the cost and/or schedule baseline.
B. Risk responses protect the time and investment of the project.
C. Risk responses may take time and money to implement.
D. Baselines should not be updated, but refined through versions.

30 Ned is the project manager of the HNN project for your company. Ned has asked you to help him complete some probability distributions for his project. What portion of the project will you most likely use for probability distributions?
A. Bias towards risk in new resources
B. Risk probability and impact matrixes
C. Risk identification
D. Uncertainty in values such as duration of schedule activities

31 Lamont is the project manager of a project that has recently finished the final project deliverables. The project customer has signed off on the project deliverable and Lamont has a few administrative closure activities to complete. In the project, there were several large risks that could have wrecked the project but Lamont and his project team found some creative methods to resolve the risks without affecting the project costs or project end date. What should Lamont do with the risk responses he identified during the project's monitoring and controlling process?
A. Include the risk response in the project risk management plan.
B. Include the responses in the project management plan.
C. Nothing. The risk responses are included in the project's risk register already.
D. Include the risk responses in the organisation's lessons learned database.

2 Given the data below:

A	0.55	-10,000
B	0.40	-65,000
C	0.30	-90,000
D	0.60	-25,000
E	0.45	-30,000
F	0.70	-245,000

What will be the expected monetary value of Risk C?
A. -$113,750
B. $175,000 if the risk event actually happens
C. -$175,000
D. -$27,000

3 A Work Breakdown Structure can be an important input to:
A. Risk Response Planning
B. Quantitative Risk Analysis
C. Qualitative Risk Analysis
D. Risk Identification

4 All of the following strategies are tools and techniques of Risk Response Planning used to reduce or control risk except?
A. Mitigation
B. Simulation
C. Avoidance
D. Acceptance

5 You are constructing a probability/impact risk rating matrix for your project. Which of the following is true?
A. The PI matrix multiplies the risk's probability by the cost of the impact to determine an expected value of the risk event.
B. The PI matrix multiplies the risk's probability scales, which fall between 0.0 and 1.0, and the risk's impact scales to determine a risk score.
C. The PI matrix multiplies the risk's probability by the expected value of the risk event to determine the risk impact and assign a risk score based on a predetermined threshold.
D. The PI matrix multiplies the risk's probability scales and the risk's impact scales, which fall between 0.0 and 1.0, to determine a risk score.

6 A contingency plan is:
A. A planned response that defines the steps to be taken if an identified risk event should occur
B. A workaround
C. A comprehensive listing of many possible risks that might occur on a project
D. A fallback plan

37 Different or conflicting objectives among project stakeholders:
A. Should be encouraged
B. Should be ignored
C. Can make it difficult for project managers to manage stakeholder expectations
D. Generally makes it easy for project managers to manage stakeholder expectations

38 Which of the following tools and techniques are used to support risk decision making?
A. Cost-Benefit analysis
B. Cost-Schedule analysis
C. Delphi Technique
D. Risk Breakdown Structures

39 Examine the data.

A	0.55	-10,000
B	0.40	-65,000
C	0.30	-90,000
D	0.60	-25,000
E	0.45	-30,000
F	0.70	-245,000

What will be the expected monetary value of Risk A and B?
A. -$55,000
B. -$31,500
C. -$26,000
D. $31,500

40 John is the project manager of the NHQ Project for his company. His project has 75 stakeholders, some of which are external to the organisation. John needs to make certain that he communicates about risk in the most appropriate method for the external stakeholders. Which project management plan will be the best guide for John to communicate to the external stakeholders?
A. Risk Response Plan
B. Risk Management Plan
C. Communications Management Plan
D. Project Management Plan

1   You have successfully completed a project. You have now been assigned a project which is midway into its execution. You have had to take this project due to non-availability of the current project manager due to health. This is a complex project involving multiple contractors and teams at various geographical locations. You decide to look up the requirements of the types of reports and frequency of sending them. Where would you find this information?
A. Project Management Plan
B. Scope Management Plan
C. Communication Management Plan
D. Stakeholder Analysis

2   All of the following are always inputs to the risk management process EXCEPT:
A. historical information.
B. lessons learned.
C. work breakdown structure.
D. project status reports.

3   You are managing a project constructing a bridge over a river. All of the risks have been identified and the design phase is just completed. The team is in its second week of actual construction. One of the subject matter experts reports that there is a possibility of the monsoons to be heavier this year. She points out that the load bearing plates earlier designed may have to be redesigned considering the additional water pressure expected because of additional rain water. What would be your best immediate course of action?
A. Schedule an emergency meeting with all stakeholders to discuss this risk
B. Risk mitigation by immediately redesigning the load bearing plates
C. Write up a change and submit to the Change Control Board for approval
D. Update the Risk register to add this risk along with its probability and impact

4   Which possible parent level RBS category would Exchange Rates come under?
A. Commercial
B. External
C. Technical
D. Management

45   You work as a project manager for BlueWell Inc. You are currently working with the
      project stakeholders to identify risks in your project. You understand that the
      qualitative risk assessment and analysis can reflect the attitude of the project team
      and other stakeholders to risk. Effective assessment of risk requires management of
      the risk attitudes of the participants. What should you, the project manager, do with
      assessment of identified risks in consideration of the attitude and bias of the
      participants towards the project risk?
      A. Evaluate and document the bias towards the risk events
      B. Evaluate the bias through SWOT for true analysis of the risk events
      C. Document the bias for the risk events and communicate the bias with management
      D. Evaluate the bias towards the risk events and correct the assessment accordingly

46   You are managing the design and construction of a public water supply annex. Tests
      indicate contaminants in the water likely from your activities. You are told there is an
      extremely low risk for causing any sickness. As project manager, what should you do
      NEXT?
      A. Inform the public that a detailed examination has been ordered to determine the
      extent to which the problem exists
      B. Do nothing because there is extremely low risk for sickness except for some effects
      on small children and the elderly
      C. Tell the public there is no problem, except for small children and the elderly who
      need to boil the water before drinking
      D. Educate the public about the advances on water treatment technology and the
      industry efficiency and safety record

47   Frank is discussing his project with a colleague and is describing his risk response
      strategy. He is happy that the risk response strategy is working well but is concerned
      that he has introduced some new risks to the project based on the strategy. What is
      Frank describing?
      A. Contingency plans
      B. Secondary risk
      C. Residual risk
      D. Risk response

8   Ben works as a project manager for the MJH Project. In this project, Ben is preparing
    to identify stakeholders so he can communicate project requirements, status, and
    risks. Ben has elected to use a salience model as part of his stakeholder identification
    process. Which of the following activities best describes a salience model?
    A. Influence/impact grid, grouping the stakeholders based on their active involvement
    ("influence") in the project and their ability to affect changes to the project's planning or
    execution ("impact").
    B. Grouping the stakeholders based on their level of authority ("power") and their
    active involvement ("influence") in the project.
    C. Grouping the stakeholders based on their level of authority ("power") and their level
    or concern ("interest") regarding the project outcomes.
    D. Describing classes of stakeholders based on their power (ability to impose their
    will), urgency (need for immediate attention), and legitimacy (their involvement is
    appropriate).

9   You are preparing to complete the quantitative risk analysis process with your project
    team and several subject matter experts. You gather the necessary inputs including
    the project's cost management plan. Why is it necessary to include the project's cost
    management plan in the preparation for the quantitative risk analysis process?
    A. The project's cost management plan can help you to determine what the total cost
    of the project is allowed to be.
    B. The project's cost management plan provides direction on how costs may be
    changed due to identified risks.
    C. The project's cost management plan provides control that may help determine the
    structure for quantitative analysis of the budget.
    D. The project's cost management plan is not an input to the quantitative risk analysis
    process.

0   Risk are documented and periodically updated using some standard tools. Which of
    the following is a method that can be used?
    A. SWOT analysis
    B. Brainstorming techniques
    C. Risk register
    D. Interviewing techniques

Answers

1   D   This is an example of a communication management plan. The questions ask 'Which project management plan will define who will be available to share information on the project risks', the key part of this questions is 'to share information'

2   B   The key word is NEXT; a risk is discovered and the next thing to do is measure it which is the same as qualify the risk (option B). All other option refer to responding to the risk and this should not be done until the risk is assessed

3   C   This is concerned with the definition of the Delphi Technique which is a brainstorming tool and technique used in Risk Identification and Collect Requirements and is based on the anonymous participation of experts

4   D   This is a good example of risk that is affecting the project. Hence Option D is the answer

5   C   the key to this is the question and the focus is on 'meeting contractual requirements and to do this a change control system is required

6   C   The answer here is Option C, the probability and impact matric is prepared during the risk management planning process and used during the risk qualitative analysis process

7   C   As part of effective communication the project manager should always send out meeting minutes after a meeting to prevent outcome like this. That way anyone not in attendance will have an understanding of what was discussed so there are no surprises.

8   C   Brainstorming includes the various planning tool and techniques and encompasses all other risk identification tools and techniques

9   C   The Risk Breakdown Structure is displayed as a hierarchical structure, containing the risk categories and subcategories

10   B   Which one of the following is NOT an output of the risk response planning: -
- There will be risk register updates after risk response planning
- The Project document will be amended and updated based on findings
- The contract will be amended based on risk response planning
The option that is <u>least likely</u> to be associated with risk response planning is Option B ...

11   D   This is an example of creating the risk management plan with a focus on understanding risk attitudes. This is the core tool and technique to be used here

12   C   Option C is the definition of a workaround

3　B　Not an easy question as it involves interpretation. The way this should be answered is the NEXT BEST thing to do and this involves working with the team. Remember that the scope baselines include the requirements, the WBS and WBS dictionary so all the information is present to make an informed judgement with the team

4　B　Risk Exposure = Risk Probability x Risk Impact

The Best Option here is Option B

5　C　Party B is only required to deliver what is defined in the contract.

6　B　The simple link here is the mentioning of the word decision in the question with the tool and technique in choice B. Decision Trees and a means of presenting the various options, associated probability and then cost (or value) impacts. Choice A and D are associated with Quantitative risk analysis whereas the risk matrix is a qualitative irks analysis tool

7　B　Performance Reports should include the following:
- Analysis of past performance
- Current status of risks and issues
- Work completed during the reporting period
- Work to be completed during the next reporting period
- Summary of changes approved in the period
- Results of variance analysis
- Forecasted project completion (time and cost)
Option B is too detailed for a performance report and would be part of the schedule model

8　C　This was an unplanned event that happened. Work around refers to handling of risk that has occurred but was not planned for.

9　C　The project manager needs to be proactive and act with urgency in this scenario. The best option here is C, even though it may be time consuming for the project manager, it allows each stakeholder to be informed directly.

0　D　The process they have used so far is fine, except the input of other stakeholders is needed in order to identify more risks.

1　B　Inputs to manage stakeholder engagement include: the stakeholder management plan, the communications
management plan, change log, and organisational process assets.

2　B　The key word is quickly. The status report (choice A. is too detailed for a quick look. The forecast report (choice C) only looks into the future. The progress report (choice B) will summarise project status.

3　A　This is used for unknowns, unknowns

24   D   When the following is mentioned 'complex web of actors, rules, conventions, processes, and mechanisms concerned with how relevant risk information is collected, analysed and communicated', this is an example of the structures needed for risk management to work. In other words this is call risk / project governance

25   C   The question is actually looking for a simple mathematical formula! Do not get flustered by all the numbers. The activity duration is 150 Days .So cost of leasing is 150 * 1200 = 180000, while cost of an outright purchase is 96000 + 200 * 150 = 96000 + 30000 = 126000 USD. So definitely leasing is not cheaper and purchasing the machinery is the better option. Now what is the breakeven point of a purchase - on the 96th day of usage of the machinery - the cost of purchase incurred is 115200 $ which is exactly the cost incurred if it were leased so 96th day is the breakeven point and hence the correct answer is option C. Take a breather - relax and digest the details - they are not as hard as they look!

26   C   Option B is a red-herring and is not specific enough to be considered as the answer. Both Option A and D are inputs which leave Option C as the only outputs. The key word in Option C is 'updates'

27   D   The question is about what documentation will need to be updated as an output of risk response planning: -
- Lessons learned will not be updated as a result of risk response planning at this point in time
- Risk Breakdown Structure is a planning tool and not an output of risk response planning
This leaves the technical documentation and the scope statement and the document with the most relevance to what is going on in the project with respect to addressing the risk is the technical documentation

28   C   This to a certain extent is a trick question. Risk Analysis is Perform Qualitative Risk Analysis and Perform Quantitative Risk Analysis. Hence Option C is not technically correct

29   A   Option A is the only answer that can cause Tom to update the baseline. All of the other options are describing characteristics of the risk response or the baseline

30   D   Ned is performing quantitative risk analysis which means that Ned is focused on understanding variances, trends and numeric analysis. This is Option D

31   D   When reading the question, the key part is the stage of the project that Lamont is in. The project is closing so Lamont needs to take action with regard the lessons learnt. This is option D

32   D   The answer here is the combination of 0.3 x $90,000. This is Option D

3　D　Page 86 of the PMI Practice Standard for Project Risk Management. Section D.2.1.20 Techniques, Examples and Templates for Identify Risks: Techniques: WBS Review

4　B　This should be clear in the sense that the response strategies are mitigation, acceptance, transference and avoidance. The odd one out is simulation which is a quantitative analysis tool

5　B　This is a very wordy question but the key is to identify what a PI matrix presents: -
1. It is measured on probability and impact
2. The output is a risk score (discount answer A.
3. Both the probability and impact are measured off scales (discount answer C)
4. Probability scales (generally) go from 0 to 1.0 (due whereas impact scales

6　A　A contingency plan is a series of steps to be used if risk occur (choice A). All other choices refer to other identified plans associated with the result of a contingency plan (or risk response plan) not going well (Choice B and D) or a risk register (Choice C)

7　C　A) Choice A is incorrect because encouraging the difference will lead to problems
B) Choice B is incorrect because a project manager cannot ignore the conflicts among the stakeholders. Ignoring will lead to non-acceptance of the project work and it will be difficult for the project manager to complete the work due to different instructions
C) Project managers must manage stakeholder expectations, which can be difficult because stakeholders often have very different or conflicting objectives
D) Choice D is incorrect because differences and conflicts among the stakeholders will lead to multiple instructions over the same task and getting acceptance from them will affect the project performance

8　A　Estimation tools and techniques to support risk decision making (including but not limited to prioritisation, cost-benefit analysis, analogous, parametric, and bottom-up)

9　B　The answer here is to combine Option A and Option B to give $31,500

0　C　The answer is really in the questions. Which project management plan will be the best guide for John to communicate to the external stakeholders? The answer here is Option C

1　C　The correct answer is Communication Management Plan. This Plan provides information such as frequency of communication, type of communication, who is responsible for communication. Hence this is the correct answer.

42 D Project status reports (choice D) can be an input to risk management. However, when completing risk management for the first time, you would not have project status reports. Therefore, project status reports are not always an input to risk management.

43 D The question is asking about the best immediate course of action. The first course of action should be to add this risk in the Risk register. And also adding the possible impact and risk probability. No other action should be performed prior to this. So - scheduling an emergency meeting while might sound as the first thing to do is not correct and neither making any change to the design. Writing up a change will only come after the risk is documented, its probability and impact accessed and then based on this information can you choose to write up a change request? So the firs course of action should be to Update the Risk register.

44 B Exchange rates are an external factor and hence become an external risk.

45 D The question asks 'What should you, the project manager, do with assessment of identified risks in consideration of the attitude and bias of the participants towards the project risk'. This is about understand the stakeholder's attitudes towards risk by probability and impact analysis. This is Option D

46 A Option A is the only option that deals with the scenario. There is a low risk of sickness so the project does not need to be cancelled at this stage.

47 B When risk is introduced (or new risk) as part of the risk response plan, it is called secondary risk

48 D A salience model is the classic interest / power matrix used to identify and assess stakeholders. The best option to choose in this case is Option D which describes exactly what a salience model is

49 C The only answer that addressed why a cost management plan would be used for quantitative analysis is Option C. None of the other options connect the cost management plan with quantitative analysis

50 C Projects document and periodically update project risk information using standard tools (including but not limited to risk register, risk database) and techniques in order to maintain a single, current repository of all project risk information.